Understanding Air France 447

Bill Palmer

Print Edition
v1.07

©2013 William Palmer, Jr.

ISBN: 978-0-9897857-2-3
ISBN: 978-0-9897857-0-9, .epub
ISBN: 978-0-9897857-1-6, .mobi

Contents

Foreword

Despite the fact that regulatory or investigative bodies have been labeling aircraft accidents as "pilot error" for years, I still feel my blood pressure rise when anyone uses that tag. To be honest, there are very few aviation accidents these days that aren't *pilot error*—the engine and airframe technology is simply so good today that systems aboard an airplane seldom fail.

All too often however, the mainstream media doesn't realize that *pilot error* is nothing more than a symptom of the accident and almost never the actual cause of the mishap. We already know the crew probably made a mistake. They were, of course, the men and women sitting in the cockpit at the time of the accident weren't they?

But *pilot error* is simply the end of the road to a chain of unfortunate events ... a road marker pointing to a much bigger problem. The real question everyone should be asking is why ... why do experienced cockpit crews often make a series of seemingly simple blunders that lead to a tragic outcome.

Captain Bill Palmer and I first connected a few years ago through the aviation-industry blog—*Jetwhine.com*—I've been publishing since 2006. *Jetwhine* exists to stimulate discussions that bring random industry people together to speculate (another word non-industry types seem to hate) when things go wrong. I remember some of Bill's comments to some of our stories, comments that made it clear early on that he wasn't simply a man with an opinion. Bill Palmer was a man who knew what he was talking about and was someone who wasn't afraid to go out on a limb putting the pieces together from which others might learn.

Jetwhine started running stories soon after the Air France accident, the first called, *Lessons From the Crash of Air France 447*, and others like, *Air France 447: The Cost of What We'll Learn*. Bill and his thoughts and ideas jumped to the forefront when *Air France 447 Pilot Error? Probably, but ...* was published in June 2011.

During the back and forth of the online conversations about those stories, Bill Palmer was there ... not just adding opinions, but adding his

i

technical expertise as an A330 instructor pilot, a veteran airline captain and as the man who'd written the A330 systems manuals for his airline. He explained the details of how things worked, as well as insights into how some systems might have added to the chaos in the cockpit that night over the middle of the South Atlantic. Sure there were people who popped up in our 447 discussions who tried to prove Bill Palmer didn't know what he was talking about, but they didn't last long. Knowledge and experience trump random opinion every time.

When Bill told me he was writing a book about the 447 accident to educate anyone willing to read it about what he believes might have happened that awful June evening, I wasn't at all surprised. I was even less surprised when he told me another goal was to once and for all explain to people how the systems aboard the A330 actually worked, as well as some of the traps any computer creates for users unwilling or unable to spend enough time to understand them in depth.

So sit back and prepare to be educated, entertained and awed, yes, awed. For within the pages of this latest version of Bill Palmer's book, *Understanding Air France 447*, readers will learn as much—or more—about the A330 than some line pilots probably know today.

By the time you've finished, you too will probably learn —as I did—*the why* behind what caused three experienced pilots aboard Air France 447, to not simply lose control of their aircraft, but to be so overwhelmed by the experience, that they were unable to regain control of the aircraft before it splashed into the sea taking 228 people to their deaths. With this volume, Captain Bill Palmer proves yet again, that *pilot error* only represents the beginning of a solid accident investigation.

Rob Mark, Evanston, IL
July 2013

Robert P. Mark is an ATP-rated pilot with both airline and private business jet aviation flying experience. He spent 10 years of his life in air traffic control with the FAA and has authored five books under the McGraw-Hill label. In addition to Jetwhine, Robert Mark serves as editor for AINSafety, the weekly online journal of aviation safety published by Aviation International News.

Introduction

On the night of May 31, 2009 Air France 447, an Airbus A330-200, left Rio de Janeiro bound for Paris. Four hours later, after leaving the northern coast of Brazil, they encountered a line of thunderstorms hiding unusual icing conditions at 35,000 feet that caused their airspeed indications to be lost. The autopilot and autothrust disconnected, and the flight controls degraded. The crew was unable to maintain control of the airplane. After climbing nearly 3,000 feet, with both engines running at full power, it plunged to the ocean below in only three minutes and eighteen seconds, killing everyone on board.

All traces of the airplane had vanished for five days until pieces of the wreckage and some of the victims were found floating in the water. Underwater searches for the remainder of the plane and the mysteries it held lasted almost two years and cost millions of dollars. In the meantime, clues emerged and theories abounded about what could have caused the loss of one of the most advanced airliners of our day.

The flight recorders and the final accident report in July 2012 by the French investigative agency BEA, revealed a shocking web of factors that may have contributed to the accident. This book will take you on a journey to understand the crew, the weather, and the unique aspects of the Airbus A330 so that you can truly understand what happened and why.

Genesis of this Book

My interest and involvement in the AF447 tragedy has been two fold: Correcting inaccurate assertions about the AF447 crash, and educating Airbus pilots.

As an A330 Check Airman for the last nine years for an international airline, this accident strikes close to home. I have spent many hours correcting errors and misstatements about how the airplane works, defining various terms in Airbus context via numerous blogs, as well as assisting other authors in their related works. Lots of folks have opinions, and they are entitled to them, but that does not make them technically correct. I felt compelled to bring a deeper understanding of the many subject areas so often misunderstood that relate to this accident.

As an instructor on the aircraft, my interest is to ensure that other A330 pilots understand the vast and quite serious issues raised by this accident. Weather and radar operation, the fly-by-wire control laws, various levels of automation, high-Mach stall, as well as training and manual flying issues are among the factors that must be understood, not only to fully grasp what happened during this accident, but also to prevent future occurrences in similar situations.

I have no ax to grind. There were many factors at play in this accident. Do not look for me to make claims of fundamental design flaws or criminal negligence. My goal is to help you understand the numerous technical aspects required to more fully understand the airplane, this accident, and the resulting reports.

This is the story of a modern jetliner that flew into the top of a tropical thunderstorm where ice crystals clogged all three airspeed sensor probes. This resulted in the loss of reliable airspeed indications which started a cascade of degradations in automation, handling characteristics, built in protections, and the ability of the pilots to cope with the situation. Each of these areas will be explored.

Within four and a half minutes of the sensors clogging, the airplane fell from nearly 38,000 feet, crashed into the sea and all on board were killed. There was no sign of the airplane for five days, and it was almost two years before the flight recorders were recovered and the mysteries of what caused this crash were revealed. What the flight recorders revealed opened up new questions, as they often do. This book aims to unravel those mysteries and search for answers to the questions.

Acknowledgments

Thanks go to my wife Mary for her encouragement and support during the endless hours of putting this publication together.

To Karlene Petitt for her encouragement, enthusiasm, suggestions, editing work, and help with promotions. To Bob Wander for moral and technical support on both content and publishing.

Thanks to those who provided expert technical information and flight narratives.

Thanks to those who read early editions of the manuscript and provided valuable feedback to help make it better.

And, thanks to my editor, Matt Cowles, for many wording, punctuation, and other finer points that nobody else caught.

Additional Resources

A companion website is available at understandingAF447.com. There you will find additional resources such as the official accident reports from the BEA, cockpit and flight data recorder transcripts that you can print out for reference as you read, and other related articles, reports, and data.

This book's appendix contains a glossary of terms, and a single-image collection of key flight recorder parameters. These items can also be accessed on the website and may be helpful to print, in order to follow along with the book.

Chapter 1: Chronology

At 8pm local Brazil time on the evening of May 31, 2009 Air France 447 pushed back from the gate at Rio de Janerio, Brazil for a 12 hour flight to Paris, France. The airplane, an Airbus A330-200, entered oceanic airspace two and half hours after takeoff, and was to remain over water and out of radar contact for a significant portion of the night.

Times listed are in UTC (Greenwich time). Local time in Rio De Janeiro is two hours earlier and in Paris: one hour later. There may be terms and concepts mentioned that you do not understand yet. Be patient. I will explain them all.

There were three pilots: Captain Mark Dubois, First Officer David Robert, and First Officer Pierre-Cedric Bonin. Though only two pilots are required to fly an A330, the flight was staffed with three to provide rest breaks due to the long flight time. All three pilots would be in the cockpit for takeoff, First Officer Robert most likely was in the jumpseat located behind and between the other two pilots for takeoff. In the cabin were nine flight attendants and 216 passengers.

Takeoff was at 22:29 UTC, 8:29 pm in Rio de Janerio.

At some point in the climb, typically by Air France procedures at about 20,000 feet, First Officer Robert left the cockpit and started an approximate three hour rest break. Captain Dubois occupied the left seat and First Officer Bonin the right.

The flight climbed to its cruising altitude of flight level 350 (FL350: 35,000 feet).

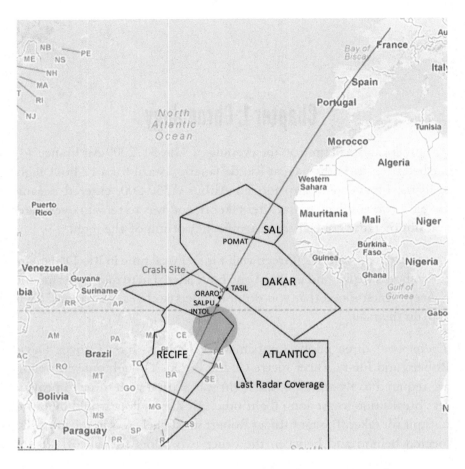

00:36 The Recife controller advised the flight they were in radar contact, and issued HF (High Frequency long range radio) frequencies for the Atlantico oceanic control center, and instructed them "Until there [INTOL waypoint], maintain this frequency."

01:14 The crew announced passing the FEMUR waypoint and stated they were contacting Atlantico on HF. The Recife controller asked them to wait until passing INTOL waypoint.

01:31 The Recife controller issued new HF frequencies for Atlantico, and a frequency for Dakar. The controller instructed them to only call Dakar after passing TASIL.

01:33 The crew attempted an ADS logon with Dakar oceanic control. ADS (Automatic Dependent Surveillance) is a position reporting system that can operate beyond the reach of radar. Dakar controls the mid oceanic area between South America and Africa. The logon failed due to an absence of the flight's data in the air traffic control management system (Eurocat) used by Dakar control. Subsequently, the Dakar controller entered a flight plan into the system. However, an error was made in the entry causing a later logon attempt by the crew to also fail. The flight would proceed by making position reports by voice over HF radio.

01:35 The flight entered oceanic airspace northeast of the South American continent with known weather in the Intertropical Convergence Zone ahead. They made a position report via HF radio with the Atlantico controller and performed a SELCAL (selective calling) check, which verified their ability to receive a call from the controller.

01:45 The flight entered an area of weather and the crew discussed their desire to climb to FL370 to try and get above the weather, but that it was too warm to climb to that altitude.

01:46 First Officer Bonin dimmed the cockpit lights, and turned on the landing lights to see outside. He noted, "It looks like we're entering the cloud cover. It would have been good to climb now, eh."

01:49 AF447 exited radar coverage as it passed the SALPU waypoint.

1:51:20 First Officer Bonin remarked "I don't have the impression there was … much … storm, not much." The captain remarked, "It's going to be turbulent for my rest."

01:56:16 The captain asked First Officer Bonin if he would be doing the landing, and if he were qualified. Bonin replied "yeah."

02:00 First Officer Robert returned from his rest break and Captain Dubois left for his. The captain did not provide any briefing to Robert other than to confirm HF frequencies ahead. First Officer Bonin was the pilot flying (PF) in the right seat, and the designated pilot in command in the captain's absence. Robert took the captain's seat but was second in command. Bonin informed Robert of the inability to climb and that there would be some turbulence ahead like they had recently encountered.

02:01 A third ADS logon attempt failed due to the erroneous registration information that was entered into the Eurocat system.

02:02–02:07 The airplane experienced light turbulence of between 1.1 and 1.25 g's.

02:06 The two first officers informed the cabin crew that it was going to be turbulent two minutes ahead.

02:07–02:10 The turbulence was borderline moderate, up to 1.5 g's. Even with the autopilot on the bank angle varied between about 3° right and 5° left.

02:08 First Officer Robert adjusted the radar gain setting to increase its sensitivity and suggested a deviation to the left of course. They turned the airplane 12° left of the planned track to avoid the worst of the weather.

02:09:46 The flight encountered an updraft. A sound typical of ice crystals hitting the fuselage was heard. Bonin reduced the cruise speed from Mach .82 to Mach .80, which is the recommended speed for turbulence penetration. The engine speed automatically reduced from 100% N_1 to 84%.

02:10:00 The updraft intensified as the airplane pitched down from 2° to 0° to maintain altitude; the autothrust system reduced thrust in order to maintain the aircraft's speed.

02:10:05 The pitot tubes (the airspeed measurement probes) clogged with ice crystals and the left side indicated airspeed fell from 275 to 60 knots but remained displayed on the PFD (Primary Flight Display). The indicated airspeed[1] on the standby instrument fell from 275 to 139 then rose to 223 knots. The right side displays are not recorded, but it is likely that they suffered similar degradations. The autopilot disconnected and the flight director bars disappeared. The airplane's flight control law changed from Normal to Alternate 2, shutting down many of the built-in protections and increasing the sensitivity to roll inputs.

Due to the loss of indicated airspeed, internal altimeter corrections were automatically recalculated as if the airplane were flying at the lower speeds. This resulted in false indications of a decrease in altitude of about 300 feet and a downward vertical speed approaching 600 feet per minute.

02:10:07 Bonin said, "I have the controls." The airplane rolled right and Bonin, the Pilot Flying (PF), began hand flying the airplane and made nose up and left roll inputs.

02:10:08 The autothrust disconnected and went into thrust-lock mode, freezing the power setting at 83% N_1 until a pilot assumed manual control of the thrust levers.

02:10:10 The pitch attitude rose from 0° to 6° and the vertical speed increased through 1,800 feet per minute. The g load, due to the pull up, reached 1.6 g's and the stall warning alerted briefly.

The PF struggled to regain control over the bank angle and overcontrolled the roll input with a series of ten alternating left and right banks. The control inputs were exactly out of phase with the roll motion. Peak bank angle and opposite lateral stick input each occurred at the same time. The roll gradually came under control over the next 30 seconds.

02:10:13 The airspeed on the standby instrument decayed again, and over the next four seconds fell from 270 to 73 knots.

02:10:17 The flight directors appeared for four seconds and directed a return to the cruise altitude.

---

1   The indicated airspeed is the airspeed that shows on the airspeed indicator. As altitude increases, this value decreases in comparison to the actual speed through the air.

02:10:20 The pitch continued to increase through 11°, and vertical speed increased through 6,000 feet per minute as the flight directors disappeared again. These pilot inputs were excessive and incompatible with the recommended airplane handling practices for high altitude flight.

02:10:23 Thrust lock was deactivated with an autothrust disconnect button despite the ECAM instructions to do so by moving the thrust levers. The thrust levers remained in the climb detent. (The ECAM, Electronic Centralized Aircraft Monitor, displays the fault messages and procedures for dealing with them.) The engine speed increased to 104% within 12 seconds.

02:10:26 The aircraft's vertical speed reached its maximum of 6,900 feet per minute, as the airplane passed 36,000 feet with a pitch attitude of 12°.

02:10:27 The flight directors reappeared. This time, they had switched from altitude hold mode to provide guidance for maintaining the current heading and vertical speed, which at the time was a 6,000 feet per minute climb.

First Officer Robert instructed Bonin to watch his speed. Bonin replied, "okay, okay, I'm going back down."

Some nose down inputs were made, pitch reduced slightly and thrust was reduced. But the pitch attitude remained well above normal and the airplane continued to climb.

Robert said, "Go back down. According to that we're going up. According to all three you're going up, so go back down."

Bonin replied, "Okay," and again Robert said, "You're at … go back down."

02:10:32 The pitch attitude was reduced to about 10° and the vertical speed decreased to 4,000 feet per minute as the airplane climbed through 37,000 feet. The angle of attack, typically at 2.5° for cruise, had so far remained below about 4°.

02:10:36 The flight director bars disappeared again. The airspeed on the left side displayed correctly, indicating 223 knots. Fifty knots of airspeed had been lost in the climb from the time the autopilot disconnected 31 seconds earlier. The standby instrument's airspeed remained abnormally low (the right side display is unknown).

02:10:42 The flight directors reappeared for one second. They provided guidance to maintain a climb rate of 1,400 feet per minute, the current vertical speed.

02:10:47 The flight directors reappeared for 53 seconds (until 2:11:40), again the guidance was to maintain the climb rate of 1,400 feet per minute. The thrust levers were moved back to ⅔ between the idle and climb settings, and the N1 decreased to 85%.

02:10:50 Attempts were made to call the captain back by ringing a call chime that sounds in the crew rest area.

02:10:51 Bonin continued to make nose up inputs and the pitch attitude increased to 16°. The airplane no longer had sufficient energy to maintain the flight director target vertical speed. A series of small roll movements began. Bonin countered each with lateral stick input. The stall warning triggered again and remained on for the next 45 seconds.

02:10:57 The stall angle of attack was reached and the airplane began to shake due to the stall buffet. Thrust was advanced to TOGA (Take Off Go Around, i.e., full power). Bonin continued to make nose up inputs as the airplane continued a shallow climb. The engine speed increased to 103% N_1.

02:11:00 Robert said, "Above all, try to touch the lateral controls as little as possible, eh."

02:11:04 The roll oscillations continued, 9° to the right, 16° to the left, and Bonin's inputs increased, using up to full left and right stick input to counteract them.

02:11:07 The airspeed indication on the standby instrument increased from 129 to 183 knots. The last of the pitot icing had cleared and all three airspeed indications were then displaying correctly. (The normal indicated airspeed for Mach .81 at FL 380 is about 260 knots.)

02:11:10 A maximum altitude of 37,924 feet was reached. The airplane had gained 3,000 feet and lost 90 knots of indicated airspeed in the one minute and seven seconds since the autopilot disconnected.

02:11:20 The stall warning still sounding, Robert said, "But we've got the engines, what's happening?"

02:11:22 Nose up inputs were maintained but the airplane began to descend. The airplane started to bank consistently to the right. Left stick inputs were made which slowed the rolling motion for a few seconds.

02:11:24 Robert again asked, "Do you understand what's happening or not?"

02:11:30 The bank angle increased to the right. Bonin held full left stick with virtually no effect on the bank angle. The airplane began a right turn that would bring it around 225° before it hit the water three minutes later.

02:11:32 Bonin said, "I don't have control of the airplane any more now. I don't have control of the airplane at all."

02:11:38 Robert said, "Controls to the left," and made two brief full-left control inputs. Bonin continued to hold his sidestick full left and moved it full aft where it was held for almost 40 seconds. The descent rate increased to 10,000 feet per minute.

The pitch attitude fluctuated between about 10° and 16° nose up, while the angle of attack steadily climbed to 40°.

02:11:42 The captain entered the cockpit. The indicated airspeeds fell below 60 knots which rendered the angle of attack sensors invalid. The stall warning silenced. As the speeds fell below 30 knots the airspeed indication was replaced by a red SPD flag. The airplane was right wing low with varying bank angles up to 45°, even though Bonin's sidestick was full left in an attempt to control it.

The captain asked, "What are you doing?"

Robert replied, "What's happening? I don't know, I don't know what's happening."

Bonin said, "We're losing control of the airplane there."

Robert added, "We lost all control of the airplane, we don't understand anything, we've tried everything."

02:11:47 The pitch attitude porpoised from 8° to 15° nose up. The thrust levers were moved to idle and the nose pitched down to about 11° below the horizon. The vertical speed increased to 15,000 feet per minute. The engine speed decreased to 58% over the next 20 seconds.

02:11:55 The stall warning triggered briefly.

02:12:04 Bonin said, "I have the impression that we have some crazy speed, no, what do you think?" He then deployed the speedbrakes and the nose pitched up level with the horizon. Robert told him not to extend the speedbrakes and then they were retracted. The nose returned to 8° below the horizon, then pitched up again.

The airplane continued to descended with vertical speeds between 10,000 and 15,000 feet per minute as the pitch attitude oscillated between -8° and +15°.

Each time the nose pitched down the angle of attack reduced slightly (though remaining above 30°), the airspeed indication reappeared with speeds between 60 and 80 knots, and the stall warning reactivated.

The bank angle rocked between 20° and 40° to the right, accompanied by corresponding yawing motions and back and forth lateral accelerations. Both pilots and the automatic yaw damper function fought to keep the airplane upright.

02:12:10 The thrust levers were positioned to the CLB (climb power) detent and the N_1 increased from 58% to 105% in 10 seconds.

02:12:30 For the first time in a minute, the bank angle passed through wings level as it oscillated left and right, the PF made large sidestick deflections to counter every roll action.

02:12:33 The thrust levers were moved from the climb detent to TOGA.

02:12:44 The airplane descended through 20,000 feet.

02:12:45 The airplane began to roll right again, and the bank angle exceeded 40° within a few seconds. Full left sidestick was again applied and held steady for 20 seconds.

02:13:18 The airplane descended through 10,000 feet. Bonin said, "We're there, we're there, we're passing level one hundred" (10,000 feet). They had already descended 28,000 feet.

Robert said, "Wait, me, I have, I have the controls, eh." He made a left input for about seven seconds, but Bonin never released his sidestick, and a synthetic voice announced "DUAL INPUT."

Bonin expressed his shared confusion again, "What is ... how come we're continuing to go down now?"

Robert instructed the captain to see if a reset of the flight control computers could help. The captain remarked that it would not do anything, but he reset primary and secondary flight control computers, PRIM 1 and SEC 1, anyway.

02:13:36 Bonin called out "Nine thousand feet." His sidestick was still about half way back, the elevator and stabilizer were full nose up (trying to comply with Bonin's pitch-up order) and the thrust levers remained at TOGA.

Robert said, "Climb climb climb climb!"

Bonin replied, "But I've been at max nose up for a while."

Robert pushed his sidestick all the way forward for five seconds, "DUAL INPUT" sounded, and the captain said, "No no no, don't climb!"

Robert said, "So, go down" and pushed his own stick forward again while the thrust levers were pulled back to climb power. Bonin, however, continued to pull back, and "DUAL INPUT" sounded again.

02:13:45 Robert said, "So give me the controls, the controls to me, controls to me."

Bonin acknowledged, "Go ahead, you have the controls, we are still in TOGA, eh."

Robert lowered the nose to 7° below the horizon, the airspeeds displayed once more, along with the stall warning.

02:13:52 Seven seconds later, despite Robert saying he had the controls, Bonin began to pull back on the sidestick again. "DUAL INPUT" was announced, and the airplane started to pitch up.

02:14:05 The captain warned, "Watch out, you're pitching up there."

02:14:07 Robert pulled back on his sidestick, and added, "I'm pitching up, I'm pitching up." The thrust levers were retarded to idle for two seconds and the nose pitched up reaching 16°.

The captain warned, "You're pitching up."

Bonin said, "Well, we need to, we are at four thousand feet!"

02:14:16 At 2,500 feet from the surface, the Ground Proximity Warning System (GPWS), announced, "SINK RATE, PULL UP."

The captain gave permission, "Go on, pull," and Bonin enthusiastically remarked "Let's go, pull up, pull up, pull up!"

The thrust levers were moved to TOGA and a nose-up command was applied by both pilots as the airplane pitched up toward 16° again.

02:14:22 Bonin pushed the takeover pushbutton on his sidestick cutting out Robert's commands. The synthetic voice announced, "PRIORITY RIGHT," and a red arrow illuminated on the glareshield in front of Robert pointed to Bonin, who had taken control.

Bonin, still not having understood what happened said, "[expletive] we're going to crash."

The stall warning announced, "STALL, STALL."

The GPWS warned, "PULL UP!"

"This can't be true," said Bonin.

"PULL UP!" shouted the GPWS.

Bonin: "But what's happening?"

The captain commanded, "Ten degrees pitch attitude," while the GPWS continued to alert "PULL UP."

Robert pushed his sidestick forward, but Bonin was holding his takeover pushbutton down and his sidestick full back. Robert's locked out inputs had no effect.

02:14:28, quarter past midnight local time. The A330 impacted the water at a 45° angle, 16° nose up in a 5° left bank with a forward ground speed and vertical speed both at 107 knots (123 mph, 10,900 feet per minute). The airplane was crushed from below and shattered into thousands of pieces. Survival was impossible. All 228 people, who came from 32 nations; 126 men, 82 women, 7 children, and one infant were killed.

02:47–05:30 Unaware that AF447 had crashed, the four control centers working the flight communicated with each other several times and questioned the estimated times of the flight's progress, and noted that none had had radar or radio contact since 01:35. Attempts had been made to contact the flight by radio call, relay from other aircraft, ACARS messages (text messages) via the Air France Operations Control Center (which were rejected), and numerous direct SATCOM (Satellite telephone communications) call attempts to the aircraft.

04:59 Air France Operations Control Center contacted the Dakar controller; both noted their inability to contact the airplane.

05:23 The disappearance of the flight was registered and the search and rescue process was triggered.

08:22–09:09 The first emergency messages were sent by the Madrid and Senegalese control centers.

11:04 A Brazilian airplane took off to begin search and rescue operations.

June 2, 2009: The Brazilian authorities confirmed to the BEA that floating debris had been observed in the search zone.

June 6, 2009: Five days after the accident, the first floating wreckage was found. Over the next 12 days the remains of fifty victims (forty-five passengers, four flight attendants, and the captain), and about 1,000 parts and pieces of floating debris were recovered by French and Brazilian naval forces.

June 10–July 10, 2009: Undersea searches were made to detect signals transmitted by the two flight recorders' emergency locator beacons, without success. The undersea terrain in the search area was extremely rugged with variations in depth from 2,300-14,000 feet over short distances. The search for the flight recorders was compared to searching for a shoebox in New York City.

July 2009: The first interim report on the accident was published by the BEA—*Bureau d'Enquêtes et d'Analyses* (Office of Investigations and Analysis).

July–August 2009: Searches for the wreckage were conducted, including attempts to detect the underwater locator beacons (which were damaged in the breakup) with side-scan sonar and a Remotely Operated Vehicle (ROV), without success.

December 2009: The second Interim report on the accident was published.

April–May 2010: The third campaign of underwater searches for the wreckage continued without success, including deep water sonar and remote vehicles.

March 25, 2011: The fourth campaign of undersea searches began.

April 2, 2011: The wreckage was found 12,800 feet deep on a flat area surrounded by steep terrain. At that depth it is permanently dark with temperatures in the mid 30's°F (2 °C to 3°C). It was 6.5 miles from its last position transmitted by ACARS.

April 26–May 13, 2011: Beginning of the fifth campaign of undersea searches. The BEA team, made up of twelve investigators and experts, devoted itself to the localization and recovery of the flight recorders, mapping the accident site, then recovering airplane parts that were useful to the safety investigation.

May 1–3, 2011: 23 months after the accident, discovery and recovery of the Flight Data Recorder (FDR) and Cockpit Voice Recorder (CVR).

May 13, 2011: Readout and analysis of the flight recorders at the BEA headquarters began.

May 21–June 3, 2011: Continuation of undersea operations. The ship and equipment were made available by the BEA to representatives of the judicial authorities, which made it possible for them to recover the remains of one hundred and three victims.

July 2011: The third interim report on the accident was published.

July 2012: The final accident report was issued by the BEA.

How could one of the world's most modern airliners, with an excellent safety record and qualified crew, fall out of the sky and disappear?

Like any aircraft accident, Air France 447's crash was a result of a chain of events and circumstances. Remove any one of these, and the accident would likely not have happened.

The crew was unable to maintain control, stalled the airplane, and crashed within four and a half minutes of autopilot disconnection. Communication issues delayed the discovery that the airplane was lost by several hours, and added two years to the search for the wreckage.

Amazingly, no component on the airplane actually failed. But, the pitot tubes were overcome by conditions that were not anticipated, causing a loss of reliable airspeed data. A cascade of system disconnections, downgrades, and human errors followed, and the loss of the flight in this manner shocked the airline industry.

Weather, design factors, pilot competence, training, and human factors all played a part.

To understand what really happened requires an understanding of the human element, the weather, and the machine. This is what I will provide.

Chapter 2: The Flight Crew

There were three pilots: Captain Mark Dubois, First Officer David Robert, and First Officer Pierre-Cedric Bonin.

58-year-old Captain Marc Dubois had joined Air France in 1988 and at the time of the accident had approximately 11,000 flight hours, including 1,700 hours on the Airbus A330, all as captain.

He earned his Private license in 1974. While working as a flight attendant for Air France between 1976 and 1982, he earned his commercial certificate (1977), instrument rating (1978), instructor rating (1979), mountain airport rating (1980), and took the written tests for first class professional and airline transport ratings.

He flew a range of Cessna, Piper, and Beech aircraft and several models of light twin turboprops.

In 1982 he earned his 1st class professional pilot's license[2], and worked as a demonstration pilot for Intra Avia Service Company in the first months of 1983. He worked for various companies until August of 1984, and was an independent pilot until February of 1988 when he was hired by Air Inter at age 37.

While at Air Inter he received a Caravelle XII and A300 type ratings, his airline transport pilot certificate, and 1st class pilot instructor rating.

---

2   The first class professional pilot's license is no longer issued by French authorities, but it was a grade between the commercial and airline transport ratings that allowed the pilot to act as first officer on any aircraft and captain on aircraft weighing up to about 46,000 lbs.

In March/April 1997 he received his A320 type rating as Air Inter and Air France merged. In June 1998, he received a 737-200 type rating and at the age of 47 was first appointed as captain. A new A320 type rating (within Air France) was issued in May 2001.

In October 2006, at age 55, he received his A330 type rating and had an unsatisfactory line test flight in January 2007. His training was extended, and a month later he passed.

An A340 rating was added in August 2007 with a captain checkout complete in September.

Captain Mark Dubois had flown 16 trips to South America since he arrived in the A330/A340 division nearly two years earlier.

37-year-old David Robert had over 6,500 total hours, almost 4,500 hours of which was in the A330.

He earned his basic license and passed his airline pilot theory test in 1992 at 20 years old. In 1993 he received his professional pilot's license and multi-engine instrument rating. At this time Air France stopped pilot hiring and drew up a waiting list due to economic issues.

In 1997 he trained as an air traffic control engineer at the French civil aviation university, ENAC. In August 1997, Air France called and he delayed joining in order to finish his training at ENAC. In July 1998, age 26, he started training at Air France and earned an A320 type rating in November of that year. His airline transport license was issued in April 2001.

He received his A340 type rating in February 2002, followed by an A330 type rating in October.

In 2005 he was assigned to Air Calédonie Internationale airline to carry out flights on the A330 between Tokyo and Nouméa, New Caledonia (a French owned island 850 miles east of Australia). While in Nouméa, he also flew the small single engine TB10.

In May 2008, he was appointed as a member of a core group at the Technical Flight Crew Division as representative of the Flight Crew hub.

Before the outbound Paris to Rio flight, his last A330 landing was March 9, 2009, nearly three months earlier. He flew the outbound flight to meet the recency of experience requirements to keep his dual A330/A340 rating up to date.

David Robert had flown 39 trips to South America since arriving in the A330/A340 division seven years earlier.

32-year-old Pierre-Cédric Bonin, was the least experienced pilot of the three. He had slightly less than 3,000 hours total time and 800 hours on the A330.

He received his private pilot license and passed his airline transport theory test in 2000, and his professional pilot's license, multi-engine instrument type rating, and glider pilot's license in 2001 at age 22.

He was selected by Air France in October 2003 and started training at the Amaury de la Grange flying school in Merville, France.

He received his A320 type rating in 2004, and his airline transport license in August 2007.

He finished his A340 type rating June 2008, and his A330 type rating followed in December 2008.

Pierre-Cédric Bonin had performed five trips to South America since arriving in the A330/A340 division one year earlier.

Nine flight attendants and 216 passengers were also on board, including First Officer Bonin's wife and an off-duty flight attendant reportedly accompanying Captain Dubois.[3]

The Layover

After the flight from Paris, the crew had a three day layover in Rio De Janerio. While that may seem like it would be plenty of time to get adequate rest for the return flight, fighting fatigue on international flights that span multiple time zones is a challenge.

Could fatigue have been a factor in the crews inability to figure out what the problem was and solve it? Possibly. A 1997 study concluded that 17 hours awake is equivalent to a .05% blood-alcohol level.[4]

The flight pushed back for a twelve hour flight at 8pm local time, 11pm in Paris. No matter how you look at it, it was a long flight on the back side of the clock. It is not easy to flip your body clock over by 12 hours to simply sleep all day, in order to work all night. The presence of three pilots on the two-pilot airplane and an on-board rest facility are a testament to that, though not a complete solution.

The French investigative TV program *Pièces à Conviction* (French for "incriminating evidence"), in an analysis of Air France 447, claimed that Captain Dubois and a female friend and First Officer Bonin and his wife spent their three day layover in Rio together. The captain's fatigue state was described by a guide, who accompanied them in a helicopter they chartered a few hours before the fatal flight, as being so tired that he was probably not fit to fly. The program also said that remarks were made that they would be able to rest on the plane.

The French news magazine *Le Point* released a story on March 15, 2013 based on a previously undisclosed judicial report that included a voice recorder conversation not included in the official accident report. The magazine revealed a comment made by Captain Dubois at

---

3   http://abcnews.go.com/blogs/headlines/2012/06/
was-air-france-captain-with-a-woman-when-flight-447-was-in-trouble/
4   Fatigue, alcohol and performance impairment *Nature*, Volume 388, 17 July 1997, page 235

01:04, "I didn't sleep enough last night. One hour—it's not enough."[5] It also claimed that the two first officers were also dangerously tired. In his book *Air Crashes and Miracle Landings*, Christopher Bartlett states "it has been said that Air France pilots regarded the long flight back to France as a good chance to have a good rest and recuperate after having fun in Rio de Janeiro."

The above allegations fall short of what I would consider as factual evidence. One must question a tour guide's qualifications to determine the captain's fitness to fly. The BEA reports did not comment on the activities of the layover, or the duration of it, concluding that the private lives of the pilots were out of the scope of the investigation. But these publications do raise the legitimate question if fatigue could have been a contributing factor to the crew's inability to properly diagnose and maintain control of the situation.

About an hour before the autopilot disconnected, the captain offered First Officer Bonin an opportunity to take a nap. One must assume that he had some reason to offer this, such as looking or behaving tired. The captain said, "Try maybe to sleep twenty minutes when he comes back or before if you want." Bonin turned down the offer. "Oh … that's kind" he said. "For the moment I don't feel like it, but if I do feel like it, yeah."

One might tend to conclude that Bonin clearly said he was not tired. After all, they had only pushed back three hours earlier. But the captain follows up with, "it'll be a lot for you." Thus apparently knowing and trying to convince Bonin that he had already had a long day and was probably not well rested.

As the flight progressed toward a line of thunderstorms in the intertropical convergence zone, clear thinking, their skills as pilots, and their understanding of the A330 would soon be required.

---

5   http://www.lepoint.fr/societe/crash-du-rio-paris-la-fatigue-des-pilotes-a-ete-cachee-15-03-2013-1640312_23.php

Rest Breaks

The question is often asked, why was the captain taking a break then?

For long flights, additional crew members are provided so that no pilot is on flight duty for more than 8 hours. This was the case with AF447, where the flight time was scheduled at 12 hours 45 min. There were two first officers, each fully qualified to act as the pilot in command in the captain's absence. Obviously, the captain did not suspect that the first officers would become overwhelmed and crash the plane within minutes of his departure.

While qualifications and experience among pilots vary, it is a mistake to assume that the captain is always the most qualified or experienced. All pilots go through the same certification course on the airplane, and captains and first officers are trained together.

It is not uncommon for a first officer to have more experience on a particular plane than the captain. In fact, that was the case with AF447. First Officer David Robert, who would replace the captain in the left seat when the captain went on break, had 4479 hours in the A330, over 2.5 times as much as the captain, though slightly more than half as much total fight time.

Pierre-Cédric Bonin, the pilot flying in the right seat, at 32 years old was 5 years younger than Robert, and 26 years younger than Captain Dubois. He had 2936 total flight hours and 807 hours on the A330 with a type rating issued six months before the accident. All three pilots had flown the A320 prior to the A330 and A340 for several years, so Airbus flight controls and handling were nothing new to any of them. In fact, their A330 and A340 type ratings courses were *differences training* from the A320 type rating they each held prior to flying the A330 and A340.

It is often asked, "why was the junior pilot flying the plane?" The fact is that all pilots need to keep their qualifications current (takeoffs and landings) and the actual flying is shared pretty much equally. No pilot would have any business being there if he was not qualified to fly the airplane at any time.

Prior to the captain going on his rest break, he discussed that First Officer Bonin would be doing the landing, and thus was to be the pilot flying at that point. According to Air France procedures at the time, because he was the pilot flying in the right seat, he would assume command in the captain's absence.

At a press conference on July 29, 2011, the BEA presented the 3rd interim report. It was asked, "You said that the captain had not clearly defined the task-sharing when leaving the cockpit. Did he hand over command of the airplane to the pilot in the right-hand seat? Also, do you understand why the more experienced co-pilot in the left-hand seat did not take back control of the airplane?"

Alain Bouillard, Investigator in Charge at the BEA, responded that on his departure, the captain implicitly designated the pilot flying who was on the right as his relief. "It is always the co-pilot flying who relieves the captain."[6]

First Officer Robert was to take the captain's place in the left seat. No particular briefing was conducted by the captain to designate who would serve as pilot in command (PIC) as this was apparently implied by the normal procedures. (Air France later revised their policy so that the left seat pilot would be the designated PIC.)

Typically, the pilots on a long international flight with an additional pilot will divide the flight time to achieve equal break times. Often times the third pilot (occupying the cockpit jumpseat for takeoff) will take the first break, followed by the captain, and then the other first officer for the third break. This schedule is not set in stone, but is common, and it appeared to be the case for AF447. The cockpit voice recording only covers the last 2 hours and 5 minutes so we only know for sure who was in what seat at the first break changeover. It is possible that First Officer Robert was in the right seat for takeoff before he took the first break. Even if that were true, it is insignificant.

According to Air France policy, the augmented crew members are present in the cockpit and actively monitor the flight from the departure

---

6   http://www.bea.aero/en/enquetes/flight.af.447/questions29juillet2011en.php

briefing to FL200 and from the arrival briefing to the gate. Outside of these flight phases, each member of the flight crew must be able to rest for at least an hour and a half continuously during the flight duty time. The captain sets the procedures for each member of the crew taking their rest.

The A330 pilot rest area is a small room located right behind the cockpit. Its forward wall adjoins the cockpit's aft wall. The rest area has two bunks to allow the resting pilot to sleep (or two resting pilots for long flights with a double crew). A dedicated button on the left side of the cockpit overhead panel rings a call chime in the rest area. (There are other call buttons for other areas of the aircraft as well).

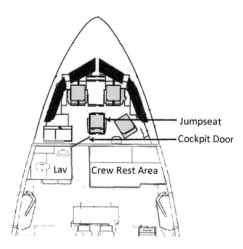

Many A330s have an interphone handset in the rest area that allows for voice communication between the cockpit and the rest area. A conversation with the captain is only seconds away at any time. But the interphone in the bunk area is optional. Air France did not take this option. The best the pilots can do to communicate is ring the call button from the flight deck, and bang on the wall from the bunk. On the transcript, First Officer Robert was called in the rest area at 01:56. Four seconds later he responded with a knock on the wall (as if to say "I'm up"). But without the interphone, there is no way to distinguish between a call to say "your break is up in 10 minutes" and "we have an emergency and need you ASAP."

It was not just communication between the cockpit and the crew rest area that was difficult that night. Voice and digital communications with air traffic control also suffered.

Chapter 3: Communication Breakdown

As the flight departed the North coast of Brazil there were communications issues that night that contributed to the lengthy delay in both locating any floating wreckage (5 days) and locating the sunken wreckage (2 years).

Two communication technologies are currently in use: HF radio, and modern satellite-delivered digital communications and tracking.

Oceanic flights are often outside the range of radar and line-of-sight VHF radio communications. To provide for traffic separation and communications in these areas, pilots and controllers use HF (shortwave) radio, and a system of position reporting at designated points along their assigned route. Pilots report their time and altitude over each reporting point, the estimated arrival time for the next reporting point, and some additional data. This system had its genesis in the late 1930's supporting flying boats (large seaplane airliners) across the Atlantic using Morse code. The HF communications now are all by voice but the medium still has limitations as a result of the physics of radio wave propagation.

HF radio uses a frequency range that can bounce off the ionosphere to provide very long range communications. However, with that capability come drawbacks. HF radio can be greatly affected by the sun, upper atmospheric conditions, sunspots, and other "space weather." Communication can often be difficult, and sometimes nearly impossible. Call quality can range from good to non-existent. Pilots are assigned two frequencies in case the first one is not workable in the aircraft's location. Because of the difficulty, pilots often talk to a radio operator whose job it is to relay messages between the aircraft and controllers, so that the controllers can spend their time concentrating on managing the air traffic. The process often involves slow clear talking, repeated transmissions, and an occasional message relay from other aircraft to complete the transfer of information.

The lack of real-time position information (like radar) limits the capacity of the ATC system in remote regions. Unlike a radar environment, where airplanes can be accurately controlled within a few miles of each other, separation in oceanic areas relying on position reports is often 80 miles in-trail and 50 or more miles laterally.

The same radio operator can cover huge areas of oceanic airspace with many aircraft, and the same frequency may be in use by pilots and radio operators on both sides of the ocean. Radio frequency congestion is often such that it can take several minutes to get a word in to make a report or request.

The transmissions on HF are often noisy and the frequencies congested; therefore, pilots do not normally monitor it full time. Instead they use a Selective Call system (SELCAL) that allows the radio operator to transmit an aircraft's unique SELCAL code. When the radio receiver recognizes its SELCAL signal it sounds a call signal in the cockpit. The call notifies the pilots to contact the radio operator for a message.

It just so happened that the night of May 31, 2009 HF communications were particularly poor. When AF447 did not check in with Dakar control, the controller attributed it to the poor state of communications that night and nobody realized the flight was in trouble until hours later.

The most modern airliners, including Air France's A330s, also use two forms of digital communications for tracking and message relay between the flight and controllers: ADS and CPDLC. Each of these technologies use cheaper and faster VHF radios when within line of site of a ground based station, but switch to satellite communications to relay the messages when out of VHF range. The satellite link takes slightly longer as the connection must be established each time, but it is often quicker than the HF system, and the messages are not subject to poor reception issues.

ADS (Automatic Dependent Surveillance) is a position reporting system. There are several varieties of this system, but the mode in question is known as ADS-C or ADS Contract. This mode requires a logon from the flight deck with the ATC facility. The controllers on the ground set parameters that tell the logged-on system on board the airplane when to make automatic position reports. The reports include the airplane's position, time over the last reporting point, estimate for the next reporting point, altitude, speed, and a handful of other data automatically gathered from the flight management system. These transmissions are completely transparent to the crew. They have no indications of what is sent or when. Their only interaction with the ADS system is to log on and log off. The logoff is usually automatic, so that the only thing a crew typically does is to log on.

Typically, the system is set to make position reports passing each waypoint along the route, a report about every 15 minutes, as well as warning messages if an airplane's altitude changes by 200 feet, route by 10 miles, or the absence of an expected position report.

The crew also has an emergency setting which will force the sending of position reports every minute. This would be appropriate if a flight was diverting to an alternate airport due to an on-board emergency as they might not pass any of the planned waypoints along the way. Setting the Emergency ADS to ON, requires making selections in the communications-system menu. It is not a one-button item and not at the top of the list of things to do when control of the airplane is in question. It would be something a crew would get to once their diversion was initiated.

CPDLC (Controller Pilot Data Link Communications) is a text messaging system. With it, pilots and controllers exchange formatted text messages to exchange requests, clearances, and messages. The messages are formatted such that key content can be interfaced with the flight management system so that it can, for example, load a transmitted clearance directly into the system, or remind the crew of instructions that take effect at a given time. Pilots can also send position reports, but if ADS is in use, it is rarely necessary. A typical use of CPDLC en route would be for the crew to request a different altitude, or a lateral offset from their planned route for a weather deviation.

CPDLC also requires a logon, which is done concurrent with the ADS logon. Like ADS, an agreement between the airline and the ATC facility has to be in place before the facility will accept the logon and provide service via this method. After all, the airline is billed for this service, so the system does not accept a logon from just anyone.

Currently, the North Atlantic air traffic control agencies are initiating a program of reduced lateral and in-trail separation on routes dedicated to aircraft with ADS and CPDLC (also referred to collectively as FANS 1/A). This initiative is expected to generate greater efficiency and flexibility for both individual aircraft and the system as a whole.

AF447 was not able to log on with CPDLC or ADS that night. An error in entering the flights data into the ATC computer prevented the system from matching up the identification data transmitted from the airplane with what was erroneously typed in to the computer. So when the crew was approaching the oceanic portion of the flight and tried to log on, the logon was unsuccessful, and the crew reverted to using only HF voice communications.

The night of the accident, AF447 was in radar and VHF radio contact with the Recife controller as they left the coast of Brazil. The controller instructed the crew to contact Atlantico over the INTOL waypoint (the boundary between Recife and Atlantico), and Dakar over TASIL waypoint (the boundary between Atlantico and Dakar) and issued the frequencies for each.

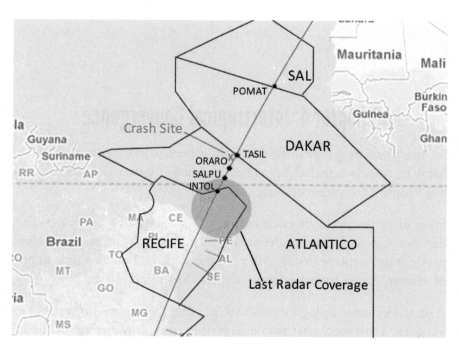

At 01:34 the crew contacted Atlantico and successfully completed a SELCAL check, which verified that the controller could call the flight. That was the last radio voice contact with Air France 447.

At 01:35 the Atlantico controller asked the crew three times for its estimate for passing TASIL. The crew did not answer, nor was the call noted on the voice recording.

One disadvantage of both HF with SELCAL, and CPDLC is that you cannot hear what the pilots of other aircraft are doing and saying. To somewhat make up for that, pilots will often communicate on a designated air-to-air frequency to exchange such information. The night of the accident other flights along the route were diverting around the worst areas of weather, but no air-to-air calls are in the transcript. The crew of AF447 was on their own to determine if a deviation around weather was warranted.

Chapter 4: Intertropical Convergence

As the flight progressed north of the Brazilian coastline, it entered a band of weather fueled by global circulation patterns known as the intertropical convergence zone (ITCZ).

Soon after the accident occurred, it was a reasonable guess that they had flown into a large thunderstorm and suffered severe damage, which brought the airplane down. After all, the airplane flew through an area of known severe thunderstorms and was lost minutes later.

A detailed meteorological analysis of the flight was done by Tim Vasquez, a meteorologist who did weather route forecasting for the US Air Force in the mid 1990's. His excellent analysis can be found at his Weather Graphics website: www.weathergraphics.com/tim/af447/. If you are at all interested in the more technical aspects of the weather, do not miss this site. Several graphics in this publication are provided courtesy of Mr. Vasquez.

Weather does play a part in this accident. The crew flew into an area of heavy weather, with only a slight deviation from course. The pitot tubes became clogged and shortly thereafter the crew was unable to maintain control of the airplane.

But airplanes have been dealing with thunderstorms and icing for the better part of 100 years, and in high altitude jets for over 50. So what happened here?

The evidence points to a unique combination of the characteristics of the intertropical convergence zone, and the specifics of particular models of pitot tube used by Airbus.

The A330-200 and -300 models were launched in 1994 and 1998

respectively. It would be 2008 before this pitot tube issue was known and well after the accident before it was understood.

The ITCZ

The ITCZ is a region that circles the globe near the equator. The zone moves slightly north of the equator in the northern-latitude summer (May–September), as it was on the night of the accident.[7] Unlike land-mass thunderstorms which are often driven by convection from below or by frontal action, the thunderstorms of the ITCZ are driven by global circulation patterns with warm moist air coming from the equatorial region. The prevailing easterly trade winds of the Northern and Southern hemispheres converge providing the lifting action required to create a storm. As with all thunderstorms, when the air rises it expands and cools leading to cloud formation.

The tropopause is the dividing line between the troposphere and stratosphere and acts like a ceiling on vertical storm development. It is the point at which an anvil head forms on many thunderstorms, as they cannot grow any higher. Near the equator, where the ITCZ is, the tropopause is typically in the 50–60,000 foot range, as opposed to 30–40,000 feet typical for the mid latitudes. The high tropopause at these low latitudes means that the storms can grow to great heights leaving little prospect of flying over them.

The significance of the ITCZ for aviators is that the oceanic thunderstorms within it show up poorly on weather radar. These equatorial storms also tend to produce less lightning than higher latitude storms, which may tend to mask their severity—especially at night. A moonless night and lack of lightning makes it difficult to make a visual evaluation of the storm. For AF447, the half moon was setting in the west, off the aft left of the airplane. The storm tops, by some estimates, towered another four miles above them.

Studies of storms in this region have shown a weakening of updrafts in the 20,000 foot range, which may account for the lesser amounts of

---

7   http://earthobservatory.nasa.gov/IOTD/view.php?id=703

lightning produced. Above approximately 20,000 feet ice crystals form. This shift to a lower energy state of matter (water to ice) gives off a small amount of heat which then adds to the updraft's upward velocity to reach, and often penetrate, into the stratosphere.

A meteorological analysis of the flight 447 theorizes that the thunderstorm tops reached 56,000 feet, with updrafts strong enough to penetrate the stratosphere by about 6,000 feet.

The final accident report states, "The Captain appeared very unresponsive to the concerns expressed by the PF about the ITCZ. He did not respond to his worry by making a firm, clear decision, by applying a strategy, or giving instructions or a recommendation for action to continue the flight. He favored waiting and responding to any turbulence noticed. He vaguely rejected the PF's suggestion to climb, by mentioning that if "we don't get out of it at three six (36,000 ft), it might be bad".

An enhanced satellite image, courtesy of Tim Vasquez's site, shows the track of AF447 in relation to the storm. The image was captured about 5 minutes after the airplane entered the storm. The flight path is noted as a yellow line. The small deviation from their course did little to avoid the worst part of the storm.

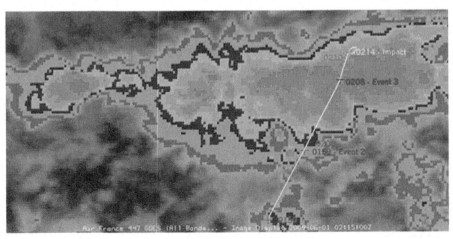

An animation is also available from the BEA which shows the deviation of other aircraft through that area, including AF459 which was on the same assigned track as AF447, but about 37 minutes in trail.[8]

The graphic below is an annotated snapshot from the animation. The deviation paths of other aircraft can be seen in blue, purple, and orange. AF447's track is in yellow.

In the minutes prior to the accident, the crew discussed the appearance of St. Elmo's fire. St. Elmo's fire appears as a glowing static discharge, often accompanied by small lightning-like discharges on the radome and windscreen. On the A330, St Elmo's fire is often seen as a hazy glowing ball on the ice probe that protrudes forward between the windshields. The ice probe is where pilots check for airframe ice accumulation because it is very difficult to see any other part of the airframe. A YouTube.com search for "St. Elmo's fire cockpit A330" will yield numerous examples of this for you to see. In my experience whenever I have seen St. Elmo's fire, turning on the exterior lights has revealed snow conditions, which can lead to the static charge build-up

---

8   The animation can be viewed in a web browser at this address: www.bea.aero/en/enquetes/flight.af.447/trajectoires/trajectoires010609.html

causing the phenomenon. At 01:37 the captain remarked, "it's snowing."

The following illustration, from weathergraphics.com, is the result of analysis of satellite and other data on the storm's profile and the flight's progress through it. Light shading is precipitation near the surface, medium shading is cloud material, and dark shading is suspected updraft areas. The green line (not part of the original image) is an approximate vertical path through the storm.

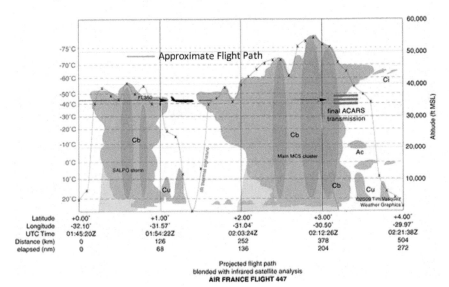

Projected flight path
blended with infrared satellite analysis
AIR FRANCE FLIGHT 447

Air France 447 encountered conditions that clogged its heated pitot tubes with frozen material. The question is "How could heated pitot tubes ice over?"

One early theory, and the subject of a NOVA television production, *The Crash of Flight 447*, was one of supercooled water—water cooled to below its normal freezing temperature, yet remaining as water. When disturbed, the water freezes almost instantly.

Supercooled water is not difficult to produce in your own freezer at home. Take a bottle of purified water and put it in the freezer. Hours later you may find the water still in liquid form, but if you agitate it, the ice crystals will grow and it will freeze solid within seconds. This can happen in the air too. If an airplane encounters supercooled water, significant ice accumulation will rapidly occur.

Many experts discounted the likelihood of supercooled water in this type of storm. Supercooled water in the atmosphere would not only have iced over the probes, but the entire airplane, and that did not happen. We know this because the A330 is equipped with two very sensitive ice detectors, and the flight data recorder revealed that at no time during the flight did they detect any ice accumulation.

One commenter on the Weather Graphics website's AF447 article provided this interesting observation: "I'm an aircraft icing specialist and wanted to point out a factor that hasn't been discussed much … high ice crystal concentrations. I've seen flight test data from power rollbacks due to flight in high ice crystal environments … In our case, the crystals collected within heated, aspirated Ram Air Temperature sensors, forming a 0°C slush …"

Seconds before the pitot tubes clogged, ice crystals hitting the exterior or the airplane are heard on the voice recorder. Ice crystals bounce off the exterior of an airplane and cause no visible ice accretion, but they can enter the probe inlets. When highly specific climatic conditions exist in combination with certain combinations of altitude, temperature, and Mach, the concentration of ice crystals entering a probe can exceed its capacity to melt and evacuate the moisture through its drain holes. The result is that the ice crystals form a physical barrier within the probe that disrupts the measurement of total pressure.

The final report states, "As soon as the concentration of ice crystals is lower than the de-icing capacity of the probe, the physical barrier created by the accumulation of crystals disappears and measurement of the total pressure becomes correct again. Experience and follow-up of these phenomena in very severe conditions show that this loss of function is of limited duration, in general around 1 or 2 minutes."[9]

---

9   AF447 Final Accident Report page 40

The type of particle that has been suggested is *graupel*. Graupel forms when tiny supercooled water droplets adhere to snow crystals to the point that they engulf the snow crystal itself.

The graupel theory is supported by the following evidence from the accident investigation:

- No airframe icing. The supercooled water theory is discounted by the fact that the A330's icing detectors were not triggered.

- Graupel has large enough particles to be audible on the voice recorder. It takes a particle with enough mass and inertia (a given density) to hit the fuselage with a sound, instead of flowing around it with the relative wind, like snow.

- Graupel has enough mass to temporarily overwhelm pitot anti-icing when concentrations are high enough. The pitot tubes are hot. But even if you put a snowball on a hot skillet it does not melt instantaneously. If there is enough mass in the blockage, and in combination with new particles being added to the blockage as the first ones melt, it may exceed the pitot tubes capability to melt the obstruction as fast as it is introduced. Graupel is of significantly higher density than snow.

---

*10 Photo placed into the public domain

- Graupel has sufficient blocking properties to prevent efficient transmission of dynamic pressure within the pitot tube. For example, water can flow and transmit pressure within the pitot tube, though it too can alter pitot-static readings, a physical non-fluid blockage could shield the pressure sensing port.

- The likely presence of snow or similar form, as evidenced by the St. Elmo's fire discussed by the crew. The accident report stated that the sound of ice crystals hitting the aircraft can be heard about 20 seconds before the airspeed loss and autopilot disconnect.

The detailed inner workings of the ITCZ thunderstorms are not well known, and the specifics of high concentrations of ice crystals within them is one of the unknown factors. Pilots routinely try to *avoid* flying through thunderstorms, so it is no wonder there is not a great deal of experience of flying through them in this area.

In regards to testing pitot tubes, the final report states:

> There are many wind tunnels around the world in which this type of test can be performed. Each wind tunnel nevertheless has its limits and its own utilization envelope in terms of speed, minimum temperature possible and water or ice crystal concentration.

> It is important to note that there are no wind tunnels capable of reproducing all the conditions that the crew may be confronted with in reality.

> Furthermore, some scientific studies are under way to characterize the exact composition of the cloud masses above 30,000 ft. They show in particular that not all the phenomena are known with sufficient precision. This is particularly true concerning the nature of ice crystals (size and density) as well as the dividing level of supercooled water and ice crystals.

Chapter 5: Into the Weather

The crew was aware of the storm before they entered it, but probably not its severity. At 01:46, about 24 minutes before the pitot tubes clogged and the autopilot disconnected, First Officer Bonin dimmed the cockpit lights to see outside and noted that they were entering the cloud cover. At 01:50 the captain and First Officer Bonin discussed their desire to climb higher to get above some of the weather, but that the airplane was too heavy for the outside temperature to do so.

At 01:51 the captain remarked, "All we needed was Mr. St. Elmo," obviously referring to St. Elmo's fire. Bonin said, "I don't have the impression there was … much … storm … not much."

At 01:59 First Officer Robert returned to the cockpit from his rest break. First Officer Bonin briefed him on the weather saying, "Well the little bit of turbulence that you just saw, we should find the same ahead. We're in the cloud cover unfortunately we can't climb much for the moment because the temperature is falling much more slowly than forecast."

After the captain left, Bonin specifically mentioned the Inter Tropical Convergence Zone to First Officer Robert and the location where they would soon encounter it.

At 02:06:05, four minutes before the autopilot disconnected, Bonin called the flight attendants and said, "in two minutes there, we ought to be in an area where it will start moving around a bit than now you'll have to watch out."

But First Officer Bonin, who was the pilot in command at the time, apparently had no thought of deviating around the weather.

At 02:08 First Officer Robert changed the gain on the radar to MAX. That will often significantly increase the displayed weather on the screen—both in quantity and intensity. It must have depicted parts of the storm not previously displayed or noticed. He suggested, "Do you maybe want to go to the left a bit? You can possibly go a bit to the left. I agree that we're not in manual, eh? Well, you see at twenty with the ..." Then "It's me who just changed it to max."

They then turned 12° left.

At 2:08:17 there was a change in the background noise of the precipitation striking the airplane. Shortly thereafter Bonin commented on a change in the cabin temperature. "Did you do something to the A/C?" He also noticed a smell, apparently concerned, "What's that smell now?"

Robert recognized the smell and answered, "It's ozone, that's it, we're alright." Then explained that ozone is, "the air with an electrical charge."

02:09:20 Robert commented, "It's amazing how hot it is all of a sudden." Twenty seconds later, the background noise changed and then intensified. The sound was identified by investigators as similar to the typical sound of ice crystals striking the airplane.

The turbulence intensified and they slowed the aircraft from Mach .82 to the turbulence penetration speed of Mach .80, and the engine anti-ice was selected on. Then at 02:10:02 the autopilot disconnected and within 7 seconds the indicated airspeed fell from 274 knots to 55 knots.

The discussion among the two first officers was ignored in the accident reports. However, it bares a striking resemblance to a first-hand account of a Northwest Airlines A330 pilot who encountered a loss of airspeed event in the South Pacific, also in the ITCZ.[11] The airplane's air conditioning system, which extracts its air supply from air coming through the engines, became overwhelmed by the amount of water in the air. It is indicative of the conditions in the updraft they were flying through.

---

11   www.flyafrica.info/forums/showthread. php?20124-Similar-event-experienced-as-AF447

The crew reported:

> Outside air temperature was -50°C SAT -21°C TAT (you're not supposed to get liquid water at these temps). We did.
>
> As we were following other aircraft along our route. We approached a large area of rain below us. Tilting the weather radar down we could see the heavy rain below, displayed in red. At our altitude the radar indicated green or light precipitation, most likely ice crystals we thought.
>
> Entering the cloud tops we experienced just light to moderate turbulence. (The winds were around 30 kts at altitude.) After about 15 sec. we encountered moderate rain. We thought it odd to have rain streaming up the windshield at this altitude and the sound of the plane getting pelted like an aluminum garage door. It got very warm and humid in the cockpit all of a sudden.
>
> Five seconds later the captain's, first officer's, and standby airspeed indicators rolled back to 60 kts. The auto pilot and auto throttles disengaged. The Master Warning and Master Caution flashed, and the sounds of chirps and clicks letting us know these things were happening.
>
> The Capt. hand flew the plane on the shortest vector out of the rain. The airspeed indicators briefly came back but failed again. The failure lasted for THREE minutes. We flew the recommended 83% N_1 power setting. When the airspeed indicators came back. We were within 5 knots of our desired speed. Everything returned to normal except for the computer logic controlling the plane. (We were in alternate law for the rest of the flight.)
>
> We had good conditions for the failure; daylight, we were rested, relatively small area, and light turbulence. I think it could have been much worse. The captain did a great job flying and staying cool. We did our procedures called dispatch and maintenance on the SAT COM and landed in Narita. That's it.

The Air France 447 investigation concluded that ice crystals had clogged the pitot tubes. But the similarity in sounds between and interior air conditioning effects between the above account and AF447 indicates that water ingestion should not be completely discounted.

In cases where the airspeed does not return to within 50 knots of the original airspeed within about 10 seconds, Alternate law is locked in for the remainder of the flight and the autopilot cannot be reengaged.

On February 2, 2013, an Etihad Airways A340-600 experienced an unreliable airspeed incident en route from Abu Dhabi, UAE to Melbourne, Australia. The incident's preliminary report[12] states:

> While cruising at FL350, just leaving Colombo FIR and entering Melbourne FIR, the Aircraft encountered moderate to heavy turbulence and experienced significant airspeed oscillations on the captain's and standby indicators. The autopilot, autothrust and flight directors were disconnected automatically. The aircraft's flight control law changed from Normal to Alternate Law, which caused the loss of some of the flight mode and flight envelope protections. The change from Normal to Alternate Law occurred twice, thereafter the Alternate Law stayed until the end of the flight. Autothrust and flight directors were successfully re-engaged, however, both autopilots (autopilot 1 and 2) could not be re-engaged thus the Aircraft was controlled manually until its landing.

Weather Radar

All of these affected flights had operating weather radar, but interpretation of weather radar requires skill, experience, and understanding of the principles involved. It is not unlike a doctor reading an x-ray. We can all find the bone on an x-ray, but it takes training and experience to discern meaning from the subtle shadows and gradients. Airborne weather radar is much the same. The radar control allows the pilot to adjust the tilt of the radar beam, the sensitivity of the receiver (gain), and the range and

---

12   www.gcaa.gov.ae/en/epublication/pages/investigationreport.aspx

brightness of the display. The colors and shapes have to be interpreted. Unfortunately the pilot does not have the option to call in a radiologist.

Pilots rely on weather radar to navigate around storms. The objective is to avoid dangerous turbulence. Radar does not directly indicate turbulence. But operating and interpreting it correctly can indicate conditions where varying degrees of turbulence are likely to be.

Radar sends out pulses of radio waves and then listens for those waves to bound back off of water droplets about the size of a raindrop.

Heavy concentrations of water droplets are often associated with the strongest part of storms, and the correlation with turbulence is quite good. The additional use of Doppler signal processing on some radar sets allows the radar unit to measure the movement of different areas of water droplets within a storm for an additional indication of turbulence, but this is generally only available at short range (40 miles).

Radar reflects poorly when liquid water is not present. It does not reflect off water vapor, the micro-sized droplets that form most clouds, and reflects poorly off ice crystals ranging from snow flakes to hail stones. Unfortunately, the upper portions of thunderstorms have fewer water droplets and more ice crystals than the lower portions and therefore do not show up well on radar.

Radar returns on the A330 are displayed in three colors on the Navigation Display (ND), overlaid with navigation and TCAS (traffic) information.

The operation of airborne weather radar is something that is unfortunately not taught very well or formally in a classroom environment. The basic principles of operation are well known by most, if not all, commercial pilots. Pilots are taught some basic tips for interpretation, but for the most part it is on-the-job training in radar operation. Few flight simulators allow for depiction of weather on the simulator's displays. Those that do are fairly unsophisticated, lacking the realism necessary for in-depth training on interpreting the subtleties of the display. It is safe to say that valuable simulator time is not spent learning how to interpret weather radar displays, even if it had the fidelity to do so.

There are many aspects that a pilot must take into consideration when interpreting a radar display. Among them are the intensity of the return (shown in colors), the gradient and shapes of the different intensities, blocking of returns by heavy weather or the curvature of the earth, and differentiating between radar returns reflecting off the ground and actual weather.

Not all areas displayed on radar need to be avoided. It is often impossible to avoid them all. Patterns of the radar display intensity and the gradient of radar returns as well as the shape of those returns provide clues as to the nature of the weather. Additionally, the altitude of the airplane and the curvature of the earth make it impossible to see storms in close proximity yet below the airplane, or those over the horizon. When determining the height of a displayed area of weather a pilot must also consider the width of the radar beam, and that ice crystals and hail (often found in the upper portions of a storm) reflect radar signals poorly.

At cruise flight levels, when storms are suspected pilots must adjust the tilt of the radar antenna beam down to look for the more reflective parts of the storm that may cause turbulence at their altitude.

Antenna gain must also be manipulated to try to enhance weak signals. The normal position of the gain control is in the "calibrated" position (center). The gain selection can increase the receiver's sensitivity to try to display weather that is too weak for the default setting, such as those within the ITCZ. The gain can also be decreased in order to concentrate on only the highest intensity returns.

Shortly after First Officer Robert's return to the cockpit, he selected MAX on the gain setting which then prompted him to suggest a deviation around at least part of the weather ahead.

Below is a typical A330 radar display on the Navigation Display (ND). Green is the least intense returns, red is the most intense returns. The airplane position, course line, and other navigation data are superimposed on the radar data. This makes navigating around weather much easier and more precise than older setups where the radar is a separate display from the navigation instruments. In this image, a 10 mile offset to the right of the active course is being evaluated. Parameters in the lower right of the display indicate the gain is being manually controlled (MAN GAIN) and the antenna tilt is 2.5° down.

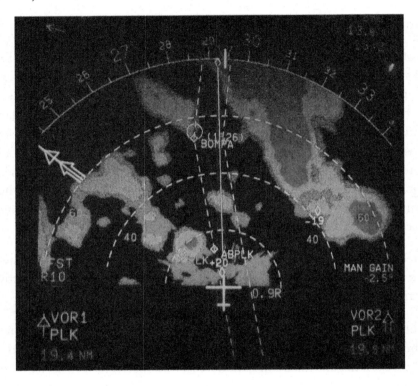

In the daytime it is often easy to see and avoid storms hundreds of miles away by vision alone. At night, moonlit clouds or patterns against a starry background may offer some visual clues. Lighting illuminating clouds from within provides a solid visual cue, but is less frequent in the ITCZ storms.

When Air France 447 was approaching the weather, the half moon was setting in the west leaving a dark sky out the window. Surrounding cloud layers prevented them from seeing much.

AF447 was fitted with a Rockwell-Collins WXR 700 weather radar.

Adjustments to the tilt and the gain are made manually. Each pilot has the ability to select a radar display range from 10 to 320 nautical miles on their respective navigation displays.

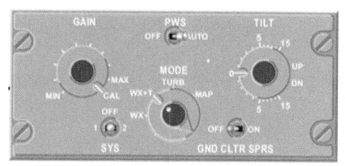

WXR-700 Control Head

A330's are equipped with two radar systems for redundancy, but only one is active at a time. Both systems use the same antenna and control head.

The WXR-700 was an excellent unit for its day and captured more than 50% of the major airline market share, but it requires manual operation.

The most recent radar units, such as the Rockwell-Collins WXR-2100 Multi-scan Radar, provide higher levels of signal processing and automatic operation. During the WXR-2100's development (about 2001 time frame) Rockwell-Collins Engineers discovered that oceanic weather is significantly less reflective than storms of similar height over land masses. A lot of time, money, and effort was put into designing algorithms to compensate for this lower reflectivity.[13] The newer units will increase the gain (sensitivity) at altitudes above the freezing level, as well as in low latitude oceanic areas to show weather that may be hidden when set to the standard setting of calibrate. Other filters and internal functions limit non-critical returns, such as low altitude weather and ground returns, so that the radar only shows weather that is a threat.

Ten minutes before AF447's autopilot disconnected, Captain Dubois

---

13   "Storm Finder. New weather radars should help airline pilots avoid turbulence and passenger injuries" Aviation Week and Space Technology, September 13, 2004

left for a routine rest break leaving the two first officers in charge of the airplane. They discussed the intertropical convergence zone, the outside temperature and the resulting limit on the maximum altitude. They called the cabin crew and told them of an area they were approaching where it will 'start moving about a bit,' to 'watch out,' and that it would be a 'good idea' to sit down.

At 02:08 Robert suggested, "Don't you maybe want to go to the left a bit?"

Bonin replied "Excuse me?"

Then Robert reiterated, "You can possibly go a bit to the left, I agree that we're not in manual, eh?" He then appeared to point out something. "Well, you see at twenty with the …" He then selected "MAX" on the radar's gain control to better show portions of the storm not displayed. It seems that the image he obtained appeared sufficiently different as to require a change of strategy. Heading mode was selected and the airplane began a slight left turn. Satellite imagery indicates that they were navigating between two heavy areas within the storm.

When possible, weather deviations should be requested ahead of time, and a clearance issued. While traffic separation may not have been considered critical at their location, because the adjacent tracks are 100 miles to the right and 120 to the left, ATC notification was still required. Pilots are permitted to make weather deviations as required. If a clearance has not been obtained with a deviation in excess of 10 miles, a 300 foot altitude adjustment is required to help avoid traffic on the adjacent track doing the same thing. The transcript reveals no attempt or discussion of informing ATC of their deviation and acquiring the clearance.

The crew's failure to operate the radar in such a way as to avoid the massive area of weather ahead of time, put them in a position of just avoiding the worst parts as they entered the line of weather. But even while avoiding the heaviest radar returns the airplane soon encountered conditions that overwhelmed the pitot tubes' ability to measure airspeed.

Pitot Tubes and their Replacement History

The pitot tube was invented by the French engineer Henri Pitot in the early 18th century and was modified to its modern form in the mid-19th century. It is widely used to determine the airspeed of an aircraft and to measure air and gas velocities in industrial applications. A simplified version appears below.

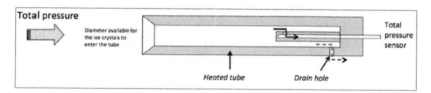

On the A330, three pitot tubes are mounted on the left side, lower half of the airplane, just forward of the cockpit. The pitot tubes are automatically heated whenever an engine is running or the airplane is in flight. This fact refutes any theories that the crew forgot to turn the pitot heat on. There was no way for the pilots to turn it off using normal cockpit controls.

Pitot Tube
(Goodrich)

The pitot tubes in use were designed to handle known icing and water ingestion issues with a comfortable safety margin. However, the standards at the time did not consider the type of icing encountered by Air France 447. Those conditions were simply not known.

It is hard to blame Thales (pronounced: tal-ess), the pitot tube manufacturer, for a design that lacked the ability to handle an unknown threat.

Nevertheless, the refinement of pitot tube designs has been an ongoing effort.

In 1995 Airbus developed a set of specifications designed to improve the performance of pitot tubes in a wide range of conditions including ice crystals. While rigorous tests were performed, the ice crystal diameter was set at a hypothetical 1 mm. However, the true size and density of ice crystals, as well as the dividing line between supercooled water and ice crystals was not known with sufficient precision, and may still not be.

In the chart below[14] the blue and red regions represent the certification requirements, and the purple and amber represent additional Airbus requirements. Below -40° all water is considered to be frozen, and therefore not an icing hazard for supercooled water.

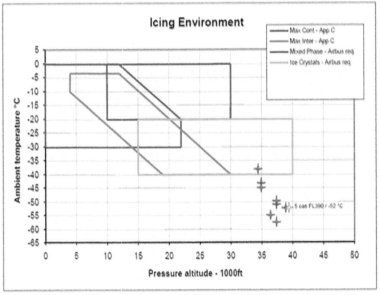

Certification Envelope of Pitot Probes

---

14   AF447 Final Accident Report, Appendix 9

In 2001 there were issues with ingestion of ice crystals and/or water with a specific model of Goodrich manufactured probes (851GR). The solution then was the mandatory replacement of the Goodrich GR probes either with Goodrich type 0851HL (HL probes) or by Thales model C16195AA (AA probes) before December 31st, 2003. Air France received its first A330s in December 2001. They came equipped with the Thales AA probes.

In September 2007, following measured speed inconsistencies observed at the time of heavy precipitation or icing conditions on A320s, and in some cases on A330/340 aircraft, Airbus published a service bulletin which recommended the replacement of the AA probes with the BA model (C16195BA). The Service Bulletin initially indicated that this model performed better in the case of water ingestion in heavy rainfall, and icing in severe conditions. Due to the absence of problems of this type affecting its long-haul fleet, Air France decided to replace the Pitot AA probes with the BA probes, but only in the event of a failure.

Between May 2008 and March 2009, nine incidents of unreliable airspeed indications were reported through pilot Air Safety Reports (ASR) for Air France's A330/A340 fleet. All occurred in cruise between FL310 and FL380. In seven cases, the ASRs mentioned the activation of the stall warning. Air France studied the events, mostly on the maintenance side. Starting in July 2008, Air France reported these events to Airbus.

The Air France flight safety officer (OSV) for A330/A340 interviewed most of the pilots who reported these incidents. The accounts given by these pilots did not suggest an immediate risk. The heads of the flight safety division, technical information office, and professional Standards for the A330/340 division also interviewed some of these crew members.

Analysis of the incidents revealed that the pitch attitude during these incidents varied from -3° to +7°, and that the maximum angle of attack was 13°. (The normal value for both is around 2.5°.) Stall warnings were momentary and no loss of control had occurred.

After the accident, six additional events, not filed as air safety reports, were found by analyzing recorded flight parameters from the fleet and maintenance reports.

Meanwhile in 2007, prompted by the earlier incidents caused by water ingestion on A320 aircraft, an exercise incorporating the "flight with unreliable airspeed" procedure conducted in an after-takeoff scenario was added to Air France's 2008–2009 training program. The exercise was considered to be representative of the main difficulties in conducting the procedure in all flight phases. However, when conducted in a low-altitude environment, the procedure calls for pitch attitudes between 5° and 15°. When conducted above the minimum safe altitude, the procedure calls for maintaining level flight for troubleshooting. There were no simulator exercises added to reflect the high altitude environment events that were encountered in 2009.

In September and October 2008, Air France asked Airbus for information about the cause of these events and the solutions. They also asked if the Thales BA probe could resolve these problems. Airbus replied that the cause of the problem was probably probe obstruction by a rapid accumulation of ice crystals, and that the Thales BA probe was unlikely to improve the performance in an ice crystal environment.

From October 2008 onward, Air France alerted Thales about the increasing problem of icing at high altitude. Thales started an internal procedure to perform a technical analysis of these incidents.

During the autumn of 2008, Air France considered that flight safety was not immediately affected by this type of incident.

Four Air Safety Reports (ASRs) relating to these incidents were published during this period in several issues of the *Sûrvol* flight safety bulletin, which was circulated to Air France pilots. On November 6, 2008, information about the airspeed anomalies that had occurred in cruise and that affected the A330/A340 fleet was circulated as an operational memo titled *Info OSV* within Air France to the pilots working in the sector. The document indicated that six events of this type were reported by crews. First Officer Bonin was about to check out on the A330 when this bulletin came out. He received his type rating in December 2008.

The *Info OSV* document stated that the incidents are characterized by losses of airspeed indication, numerous ECAM messages, and in some cases, configuration alarms. The events occurred at high altitude in turbulence, in zones in which icing was forecast or observed, for aircraft flying at a Mach of 0.80 to 0.82, with autopilot and autothrust engaged. The chronology of the anomalies was described. It stated that, "during this phase, which lasted for approximately a few minutes, the crews did not report any feeling of overspeed (vibration, acceleration) or the approach to stall (pitch attitude, angle of attack, reference to the horizon) despite the activation of the stall warning."

It stated in bold red letters "be vigilant in flight conditions of high altitude, icing, and turbulence."

Four general recommendations were included in the document. (Approximate translations)

- Read the complementary technical information carefully.
- Do not be taken by surprise.
- Identify and confirm the situation.
- Recovery in case of manual control of the aircraft. Proceed by making small corrections.

The presence of this information and the dissemination of these bulletins indicates that Air France pilots, especially A330 and A340 pilots, should have been aware of these incidents. The conditions that AF447 encountered were exactly the conditions that the bulletins and Air Safety Reports referred to.

Unfortunately, the "Flight with Unreliable Airspeed" procedure and the conditions for its application were not mentioned in the *Info OSV* document. A safe attitude and power setting to go to in the event of the loss of automation and/or airspeed indications was also not mentioned. Yet, that key piece of information is what pilots who have successfully flown through the loss of airspeed events report having used in the critical first seconds.

Training by bulletin rarely has lasting effectiveness, and perhaps even less so when the guidance is general in nature and includes only vague corrective actions.

On November 12, 2008 Airbus revised the earlier 2007 service bulletin. Like the earlier version, this version mentioned the improvement that could be provided by the Thales BA probe in relation to water ingestion, but no longer mentioned icing conditions.

Airbus said that there was no solution that could totally eliminate the risk of probe icing, that the three types of probes installed on the Airbus satisfy criteria that are much higher than the regulatory requirements for certification in relation to icing, and provided a reminder of the procedure to be applied in the event of an erroneous airspeed event.

On November 24, 2008 the issue of inconsistent airspeed indications was raised during a meeting between the technical divisions of Air France and Airbus. Air France requested an analysis of the root cause and a technical solution to resolve the issue. Air France suggested that BF Goodrich probes should be fitted, due to an appearance of greater reliability over the Thales models. Airbus confirmed its analysis and agreed to check the option of replacing the Thales probes with BF Goodrich probes.

Meanwhile, other airlines were also experiencing loss of airspeed events. It was not known what caused these events. The leading theories centered around water ingestion that was tossed around inside the pitot by the turbulence that seemed to be a common factor with each event. Many of the airspeed transients were quite short, such that in some cases the crew did not even see what caused the autopilot to disconnect. Others lasted longer (one to three minutes) with flight control law degradation effects, but loss of control had not been a problem. Looking at the flight data from some of these incidents, the loss of airspeed was so sudden that it looked like it could easily be an electronic problem.

At the end of March 2009 (about two months before the accident), Air France experienced two additional events involving the temporary loss of airspeed indication, including their first one on an A330.

On April 3, 2009, in light of these two new cases, Air France once again asked Airbus during a technical meeting to find a definitive solution. On April 15, Airbus informed Air France of the results of a study conducted by Thales. Airbus stated that the icing phenomenon involving ice crystals was a new phenomenon that was not considered in the development of the Thales BA probe, but that probe still appeared to offer significantly better performance in relation to unreliable airspeed indications at high altitude. Airbus offered Air France an "in-service evaluation" of the BA standard to check the behavior of the probe under actual conditions.

Air France decided to extend this measure immediately to its entire A330/A340 long-haul fleet, and to replace all the airspeed probes. On April 27, 2009 (32 days before the accident) an internal technical document was drawn up to introduce these changes . The modification work on the aircraft was scheduled to begin as soon as the parts were received.

The first batch of Thales BA probes arrived at Air France on May 26th, 2009, six days before flight 447 crashed. The first aircraft was modified two days before the accident. At the time of the accident, flight 447, registration number F-GZCP, was fitted with the original Thales AA probes. They were due to be replaced upon the airplane's return to Paris.

As of November 2009 (five months after the accident) Airbus had identified thirty-two loss of airspeed events that had occurred between November 2003 and June 2009. According to Airbus these events are attributable to the possible "destruction" of at least two pitot probes by ice. Eleven of these events occurred in 2008 and ten during the first five months of 2009. Twenty six of these incidents (81%) occurred on aircraft fitted with Thales AA probes, two on aircraft with Thales BA probes, and one on an airplane equipped with Goodrich HL probes. [15]

Post-accident wind tunnel tests with large concentrations of ice crystals were able to duplicate the issue in a controlled environment. The Goodrich manufactured probe behaved better than the Thales probes and was therefore the eventual replacement probe.

---

15 AF447 Final Accident Report page 65

Pitot Static Operation

The pitot-static system is designed to determine airspeed and altitude by precisely measuring both the dynamic pressure resulting from forward movement through the air, and the ambient static pressure at that altitude.

The air pressure measured in a pitot tube is the combination of the dynamic air pressure plus the static pressure. To determine the dynamic component (airspeed), the static pressure must be subtracted from the total pitot pressure. The dynamic component then directly relates to indicated airspeed. That is where the fun begins, as that value must then be corrected for temperature, pressure, and errors induced by the probe's placement on the airplane to determine the airplane's true airspeed.

You may have seen photos of flight-test aircraft where the probes are mounted on long poles that project out in to undisturbed air in front of the airplane for greater accuracy. No doubt, if production airplanes had those long probes, they would be broken on a regular basis by all manners of ramp equipment banging into them. Instead, the pitot, static, angle of attack, and other air data sensors are mounted on the fuselage.

Manufacturers attempt to position the sensors so that they can be reasonably accurate throughout the range of the airplane's operating envelope. This can be quite challenging, as airflow around the fuselage changes quite a bit throughout an aircraft's speed range. Sometimes the outputs of additional sensors, such as accelerometers, are used to tweak the air data to avoid erroneous readings.

Static ports are located to get an accurate measurement of the outside atmospheric pressure. But the ports have little choice but to be mounted on the fuselage somewhere, subject to local pressure differences as air flows around the complex exterior of the airplane. Almost all airplanes have some error due to the position of the static ports. These errors are carefully recorded during flight testing. The manufacturers provide a correction table and in the case of modern airplanes like the A330, build the corrections into the air-data computer software, so that the values displayed to the pilot are accurate.

The value of the measured static pressure must be corrected for this error before being used to calculate other parameters such as airspeed. The value of the correction depends in particular on the Mach, and takes into account the position of the sensors on the fuselage. Therefore, the correction performed for each static port is slightly different.[16]

For each airspeed system, the calculation principle is as follows:

Knowing Pt (total pitot pressure) and Ps (static pressure) makes it possible to calculate a Mach value used to correct the Ps. The corrected Ps is then used to calculate the CAS (calibrated airspeed) and the standard altitude.

With the known Mach value, the total air temperature (TAT) measurement makes it possible to determine the static air temperature (SAT), which in turn makes it possible to calculate the true air speed (TAS).

The corresponding IR (Inertial Reference) unit then uses the true air speed to calculate the wind speed from its own internal ground speed and track values. It also uses the derivative of the standard altitude value that it combines with the integration of the vertical accelerations to calculate the vertical speed, known as baro-inertial (Vzbi), which is then displayed on the PFD.

---

16   AF447 Final Accident Report page 40

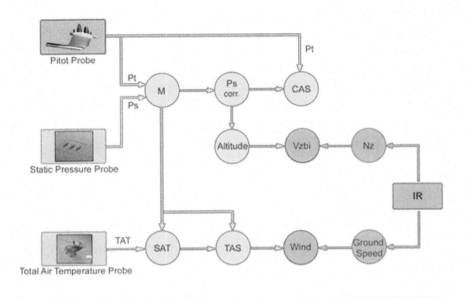

CAS : Calibrated Airspeed - speed *indicated on the PFD*
TAS : True Airspeed - *aircraft velocity relative to the air mass*
M : Mach Number - ratio between true airspeed and sound velocity
Ps : Static Pressure - *pressure of outside air*
Pt : Total Pressure - *static pressure added to the pressure due to aircraft speed*
SAT : Static temperature - *outside air temperature*
TAT : Total Temperature - *static temperature added to the temperature due to aircraft speed*
Vzbi : Baro-Inertial Vertical Speed
Nz : Vertical Load Factor

BEA

The A330 static ports are located below the fuselage mid-line forward of the wing. On the A330-200 in particular, as a result of the position of the static pressure sensors, the measured static pressure overestimates the actual static pressure. One of the first effects after AF447's pitot tubes became obstructed was that internal altimeter corrections were recalculated as if the airplane were flying at the lower speeds. This resulted in false indications of a 300 foot decrease in altitude and a downward vertical speed approaching 600 feet per minute.

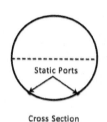

Static Ports

Cross Section

Static Ports

The pitot icing lasted for about a minute and five seconds. But 30 seconds later the airspeed indications again fell to extremely low levels.

Consider that in normal operation, the angle of the airflow along the fuselage is no more than a few degrees. At 02:11:45, as the airplane was descending through 35,000 feet, the angle of attack started to exceed 45° on a regular basis. At the same time the indicated airspeed fell to values that were well below its actual forward speed. If it were only a matter of the air striking the pitot tube at the 45° angle, geometry tells us that the resulting ram pressure would be 70% of its actual value, but the indicated airspeeds were often below 60 knots for the number one air data system and near zero for the standby instrument.

This created a situation where the air was pushing into, in addition to flowing over, the static ports. Dynamic pitot pressure is only calculable by subtracting the static pressure component. If the air is directed at the pitot inlet and the static port inlet at the same angle then the differential will fall to zero, or perhaps beyond. This dynamic accounts for the repeated falling of the airspeed indications to invalid values.

In addition to airspeed, altitude and vertical speed indications were also compromised because of this effect. At this same time, the recorded vertical speed indications become erratic and changed at rates that had no corresponding change in the vertical g load.

---

17   Air France A330-200 photo copyright Wim Callaert

Further evidence of this phenomenon is that sometime during the 02:11 minute (the ACARS-transmitted fault reports were not recorded more precisely than to the minute) the comparison between the static and pitot pressures were "out of bounds." That is the static pressure was greater than the pitot-tube sensed pressure. This caused a hard speed/Mach function error in the standby instrument ("hard" meaning that it persisted over a period of time). In normal flight regimes this would be a nonsense situation, where static pressure was greater than pitot pressure, even if the pitot tubes were completely blocked. But the correlation of this message with a time period where the angle of attack became consistently excessive lends credence to the explanation that the angle of attack was responsible for the airspeed values at ridiculously low readings, long after the icing issue ceased to exist.

Airspeed vs. Angle of Attack

There have been many calls for the installation of angle of attack (AOA) indications on transport category airplanes. This accident would seem to be the perfect example to make that case. Unfortunately, it is not that simple.

Airspeed/Mach is an excellent indication for a number of reasons. It provides a direct indication of limit speeds for the airframe and flaps/slats. In cruise flight, it provides a higher degree of precision for performance than AOA alone, and an indirect indication of AOA within the normal envelope. Cruise performance is more related to Mach number than AOA. Lift is increased and stall AOA decreased with increasing Mach number, even at the same airspeed and AOA.

Angle of attack indications are no panacea. In cruise, one degree of angle of attack change is equivalent to up to 25 knots of airspeed change. The stall AOA is also not a constant, at least not at Mach numbers above 0.3. Therefore, to act as a replacement in case of loss of airspeed/Mach number, the Mach number actually needs to be known to know the stall AOA, or conservative assumptions made. It is a catch-22. That is not to say it would be useless. In the case of AF447, it would have shown an obviously excessive AOA, and perhaps would have allowed the crew to answer the question both first officers posed: "What's happening?" It might have led to earlier attempts to recover from the stall with pitch. However, in so much as the pilot flying seemed to be ignoring the more fundamental indications of pitch attitude and altitude, along with numerous stall warnings, one could question what difference a rarely used AOA gauge would have made.

AOA indications are more useful at low altitudes (where the stall angle is constant) for higher AOA flight regimes like approach. Precision in the approach and climb phases is more critical and an AOA reference is appropriate from a aerodynamic perspective. Military jets equipped with AOA indications use them in those flight phases and high performance maneuvering, but not at high-altitude cruise. The military attitude/AOA critical carrier approach also uses a "back side of the power curve" technique not compatible with transport category flight director and autothrust operating.[18] Additionally, the stall AOA is also influenced by flap and speed brake position. The addition of flaps actually reduces the stall AOA.[19] Other factors such as CG, required body angle clearances, gust factors, and minimum control speeds (not AOA related), combine so that no single AOA can be targeted to ensure proper speed or landing attitude margins.

Measuring AOA is also more complicated than it may first appear. The airflow around the fuselage, where transport airplane angle-of-attack vanes are mounted, is not identical with the airflow experienced at the wing. Boeing cites Mach number, flap and gear position, side-slip angle, pitch rate, ground effect, fuselage contour, radome damage, installation error, sensor inaccuracies, contamination, and damage among the factors that add errors to the measurement of AOA.

Some transport category aircraft do have AOA indications (e.g., late models of B-737, 767, and 777). The indication provides a green approach band which represents the normal range for approach operations. The band is intended not as a target reference for the approach, but a tool to detect configuration errors, reference-speed calculation errors, and

---

18   www.boeing.com/commercial/aeromagazine/aero_12/attack_military.html
19   www.boeing.com/commercial/aeromagazine/aero_12/attack_story.html

very large errors in gross weight, as not all approach speed parameters are related to or sensed by AOA.

Airbus does offer an angle-of-attack based speed replacement display called the Back Up Speed Scale (BUSS). The BUSS provides a green target area based on angle of attack and replaces the barometric altitude display with GPS altitude data. However the display only comes on after all three ADRs (Air Data Reference units) are shut off by the pilot, and its use is not recommended above 25,000 feet.

Boeing notes an additional hazard: "Pulling to stick shaker AOA from a high-speed condition without reference to pitch attitude can lead to excessive pitch attitudes and a higher probability of a stall as a result of a high deceleration rate."

For a more complete discussion of these AOA integration issues for transport airplanes, see the excellent issue of Boeing AERO magazine at: http://www.boeing.com/commercial/aeromagazine/aero_12/attack_story.html

As part of the investigation's certification recommendations, the BEA recommended that "EASA (the European Aviation Safety Agency) and the FAA evaluate the relevance of requiring the presence of an AOA indicator directly accessible to pilots on board airplanes."

I think it is indicative of the complexity of the issue that the agency that does not concern itself with the cost or technological barriers associated with many of its recommendations has only called for the evaluating the relevance of AOA indicators, and not their outright installation.

Chapter 6: "I Have the Controls"

As soon as the autopilot disconnected First Officer Bonin announced "I have the controls." At that moment his skills and knowledge were put to the test. When the automatic systems stop functioning ('the magic goes away') and flight control laws degrade, a pilot must identify and understand the situation, and consolidate many areas of understanding into his actions. An understanding of aerodynamics, the characteristics of the A330's fly-by-wire control system, performance, procedures, and raw instrument flying skills must be applied simultaneously.

First Officer Bonin's inappropriate pitch up, attempts at stall recovery solely with power, misidentification of a overspeed situation, difficulty handling the airplane in Alternate Law at high altitude, and other failures highlight many the areas of understanding that must be fully grasped by every pilot crewmember to operate safely.

Understanding the Machine

Would this accident have happened in a Boeing? Some say no, but history does not necessarily agree.

The accident happened in a Airbus A330-200. A marvel of modern technology, without question. But the Airbus has its own unique qualities that pilots must understand to operate it properly and safely.

There is no question that the Airbus is different from any other civilian aircraft. Its flight control handling is different, its autothrust system works differently, and it has sidestick controllers instead of conventional control wheels, which is definitely different. I do not think it is a dangerous or bad design. In fact, overall I think it is a good design.

When I was learning to fly gliders, already an airline pilot at the time, my glider instructor pointed out that the glider was not just an airplane without a motor. It was in fact a whole different *category* of aircraft. Pilots will recall that the word "category" divides aircraft into airplanes, balloons, rotorcraft, gliders, airships, etc., so it is in fact a legal definition too. But while all aircraft obey the same laws of physics and aerodynamics, they have their own unique handling characteristics.

Due to a glider's long slender wings and the slow speeds that they often operate at, a glider pilot's coordination of rudder and aileron inputs can be quite different from a regular airplane. In tight slow turns, such as when climbing in a thermal, a glider pilot may actually have opposite aileron and rudder applied—a virtual sin in the airplane world. These differences are not unsafe nor difficult to learn or even master, but they are different. It takes understanding the principles involved and practice, and that is why there is separate license for each category.

I think that the different handling qualities of an Airbus fly-by-wire airplane have a similar degree of difference from a conventional airplane, as an airplane has to a glider. While not designated as its own category, the Airbus, like any large or jet powered airplane, requires training and a specific type rating for that model in order to operate it as a pilot, as it should.

These differences may have played a part in the failure of the AF447 pilots to recover from their loss-of-airspeed incident. They may not have fully understood what inputs they were making to the flight controls, or what they were really asking for. But they should have.

When everything is working right, as it is more than 99.9% of the time, the Airbus fly-by-wire system provides excellent protection from inadvertent stall, flight envelope exceedance, windshear recovery, and more. When something is not working properly it is important for the pilot to understand what has changed and that he is now fully responsible for not exceeding normal limits. That responsibility is something most pilots take for granted anyway.

Flight Control and Stalls Review

In conventionally controlled airplanes, the pilot moves the controls to directly command the position of the flight control surfaces. In most larger aircraft, and some smaller aircraft as well, the pilot is not directly moving the flight control surface, but is doing so through some mechanical means to activate a hydraulic or electric servo that moves the control.

As an airplane has a wide range of speeds, the effect of a specific amount of control deflection has differing results depending on that speed. At low speed, there is little airflow and the controls are easy to move, yet require more deflection to achieve a given performance, such as a given roll rate. At high speeds there is greater airflow over the control surface which will have a greater effect, and the same roll rate can be achieved with much less control deflection. At higher speeds the force needed to displace the controls into the faster relative wind is greater as well. These forces cannot be felt through a hydraulic system; therefore, an artificial feel system is incorporated to mimic the natural feel as if there was a direct connection.

At high altitude, a given control deflection provides a faster airplane response than at low altitude due to less aerodynamic damping (i.e., it is easier to move the airplane around in the thinner air). This creates an opportunity for over-controlling the airplane if large control inputs are made.

In pitch, there is a balance between the center of lift from the wings, the center of gravity, and the aerodynamic forces created by the tail of the airplane. The airplane pivots around the center of gravity, which is about 20-30% of the way back from the average front of the wing (the mean aerodynamic chord, to be precise). This balance is dynamic and changes with the loading as well as the speed of the airplane. The two horizontal components of the tail, the horizontal stabilizer and the elevator hinged to its aft half, move to control the pitch attitude of the airplane.

The elevator is the primary pitch-control surface and moves immediately with pitch commands. The stabilizer is adjusted to reduce prolonged elevator deflection for both efficiency and controllability. This adjustment is called trim, and the stabilizer is often referred to as the "trimmable horizontal stabilizer" (THS) or simply the "stab," and the adjustment of it as *stab trim*.

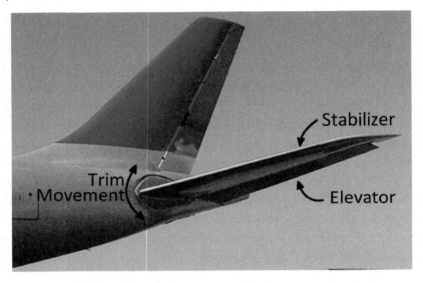

The trim setting is such that at a given load distribution, the airplane's trim setting is valid for a particular speed. If the airplane slows down, left on its own the nose will tend to pitch down, which will increase speed, causing the nose to pitch up, causing the airplane to slow down to eventually become stable at the speed the trim is set for. An airplane with this configuration, like commercial jet transports, is considered dynamically stable (it will return to its stable speed).

Therefore, if an airplane is trimmed to fly at a given speed and the actual speed falls much below that, the pilot has to exert additional control force to keep the nose of the airplane from pitching down. Either that or adjust the trim to the new speed.

When a new speed is desired, the pilot or autopilot adjusts the trim, so that the airplane is stable at the new desired speed. This occurs repeatedly throughout any flight.

An additional factor that plays in this balance is the thrust from the engines, especially when they are mounted below the wing and not in line with the center of gravity. An increase in power from below the center of gravity will induce a pitching-up moment and a new balance must be achieved with the trim.

Operation of Trim

On Airbus fly-by-wire aircraft, the trim is normally automatic. The automatic trim moves the stabilizer so that the elevator is neutral on average (aligned with the stabilizer). This is both aerodynamically efficient and it provides for a range of elevator movement, and thus control, on either side of the trimmed setting.

A trim wheel is located next to the thrust levers on the center pedestal. The trim wheel provides a direct link with the THS hydraulic control. Whenever the THS moves the trim wheel moves, and vice versa. Its operation is silent and usually goes unnoticed. The pilot can adjust the stabilizer manually with the trim wheel, and manual movement of the trim wheel control overrides the automatic function. However, except in case of a malfunction, there is no reason to do so.

Trim Wheel

But Airbus fly-by-wire airplanes are operated by a different set of rules than a conventional airplane. Those rules are called flight control laws: Normal, Alternate (with two versions), and Direct.

In practicality, the trim operation is completely behind the scenes. Trim operation in Normal and Alternate Law does not affect the way the airplane handles, which is quite a departure from conventional airplanes.

Assuming the pitch controls laws are operative (Normal, Alternate 1, or Alternate 2), the elevators will move to maintain the g-force/pitch rate requested by the pilots via the sidestick. The trim does **not** play a part in the feel of the airplane. If the pilot pitches up to 15° and lets go of the sidestick, the pitch will remain there, whether the stabilizer has trimmed or not. The only difference is how much elevator the flight control computer will command in order to maintain that attitude. As the stabilizer trims, less elevator will be held, but the pitch attitude and sidestick position will remain unchanged.

In a case where the automatic trim fails, the pilots (directed by procedure) will trim the stabilizer by referencing the flight control display on the ECAM, and trim the stabilizer until the elevator is in the neutral position. While this is done, the sidestick remains in neutral and no change is felt with the sidestick or actual aircraft pitch. Once the stabilizer and elevator are aligned, the elevator's ability to carry out a pitch up or pitch down order is assured. If this were not done, and the elevator were near the limit of its range (due to stabilizer being positioned in the opposite direction), the elevator would not be able to move further in order to carry out a pitch change. We describe this scenario as running out of elevator.

If the pitch laws have degraded to Direct Law, the elevators are directly controlled with sidestick position. If the sidestick must be held against the centering spring then trim is called for. When properly trimmed the sidestick will be in the center position and the elevator and stabilizer aligned. If other than neutral elevator is required, the pilots must hold the sidestick deflected and move the stabilizer with the trim wheel until sidestick no longer needs to be held out of center.

Stalls

There are limits to how slow an airplane can fly. The slower an airplane moves through the air, the greater amount the wing must be deflected against the direction of movement in order to achieve the required amount of lift to stay in the air. The angle between the wing and the relative wind is the angle of attack (AOA).

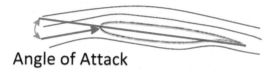

Angle of Attack

Above a critical angle (in the lower atmosphere it is typically around 15°) the air can no longer flow smoothly around the wing, the airflow becomes turbulent and lift rapidly decreases with any increase in the angle of attack. This is called a stall. The stall angle of attack is considered constant for a given configuration, but is decreased by flap extension and generally for Mach numbers above 0.3 (about 200 knots).

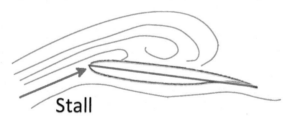

Stall

The stall is accompanied by characteristic behaviors of the airplane such as loss of effectiveness in the controls and a buffeting of the airplane from the turbulent airflow. Pilots experience this in training, albeit briefly.

In primary flight training, pilots are taught that an airplane always stalls at the same angle of attack (for a given wing configuration), no matter what the speed, weight, or attitude. That is true enough throughout the normal operating range of airplanes that pilots learn to fly in. However, that is not necessarily the case for high performance aircraft operating at high altitudes.

To recover from a stall, the angle of attack must be reduced so that the air can flow smoothly around the wing again. This is properly accomplished by pitching the nose down. However, if there is sufficient engine power available, an application of a large amount of thrust may be sufficient to change the airplane's direction of movement and thus indirectly reduce the angle of attack.

On the high speed end, there are two limit speeds to consider. The first is a straight airspeed limit that limits the maximum force on the structure from high airspeeds. The second is a Mach number limit (Mach 1.0 is the speed of sound). The Mach limit references the point that airflow around parts of the wing become supersonic, forms a shock wave, and also disturbs the flow of air around the wing, which results in a large increase in drag. The Mach number that this occurs at is the *critical Mach number*. The supersonic flow and shock wave formation is also accompanied by a buffet, known as Mach buffet. Most pilots will never experience Mach buffet in airline operations or in simulator training. For the A330, this critical Mach number is beyond the maximum operating speed imposed by other speed limiting factors.

In older generation aircraft, the onset of this supersonic airflow could also result in *Mach tuck*, a dangerous loss of control. Mach tuck is a strong pitch down force due to the redistribution of airflow and forces resulting from shockwave formation. In a Mach tuck situation the center of lift is shifted aft toward a swept wing's tips, inducing a pitch down moment. The shock wave may also reduce the effectiveness of the tail reducing its normal pitch-down moment, which may then make a pitch up recovery impossible. In the early days of commercial and private jet operation, a number of accidents occurred due to this phenomenon.

In order to allow for high cruise airspeeds, and avoid the effects of Mach buffet, airplanes of the A330's generation employ a "supercritical" airfoil. These airfoils typically have a larger leading edge radius, a flatter upper surface, and a rather distinctive cusp at the trailing edge. These airfoils were developed by NASA starting in 1965 and have improved over time.

Supercritical Airfoil

The supercritical airfoil is not "extra critical", but one with a high critical Mach number (super, meaning high). It allows efficient cruise speeds at relatively high Mach numbers before incurring a large increase in drag due to shock wave formation.

Modern aircraft with supercritical wing profiles offer numerous advantages, which include:

- Improved aircraft control characteristics at high speed[20]
- The position of the aerodynamic center is virtually stable for supercritical profiles, and therefore less susceptible to adverse high Mach effects such as Mach tuck.
- They have a higher drag divergence Mach number and greatly reduce shock-induced boundary layer separation.
- Their geometry allows for a thicker wing and/or reduced sweep angle, each of which may help reduce the weight of the wing structure.
- The increase in drag above a given speed is so great that it is extremely unlikely, or even impossible, to fly faster than the demonstrated dive speeds that ensure the absence of flutter in flight testing (typically set at maximum operating Mach +.07).

Therefore, the airfoil is better behaved at near-Mach speeds than older generation airfoils, as the critical Mach number is higher, and the buffet effects less. As a result, the threat of loss of control due to an overspeed is much less than in older generation aircraft.

Unfortunately, the characteristics of these new airfoils and the reduced possibility of Mach buffet are not well known to pilots.

---

20   AF447 Final Accident Report page 43

High Mach Stall

At higher Mach numbers, the stall angle of attack is considerably decreased. Despite the flight school admonition that an airplane always stalls at the same angle of attack, the stall angle of attack is greatly influenced by Mach number. So much so that while the airplane could pull more than 2.5g's without stalling at low altitude and normal operating speeds, at the maximum recommended cruise altitude and Mach, the stall buffet may occur at only 1.3g's. This is the result of the compressibility of the air, and it starts to become a factor at around 200 knots of calibrated airspeed (the effect is more pronounced at higher altitude).

To use the stall warning as a point of reference, at 0.3 Mach the A330 stall warning comes on at an angle of attack of about 10°, at M.82, it is only 4°.

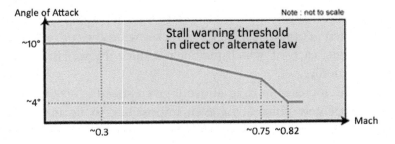

Airplanes are equipped with stall warnings to allow the pilot to correct high angle of attack situations before they become an issue. The warning intentionally comes on prior to the actual stall so that the pilot may recover. It is not necessarily an indication that the wing is currently stalled.

On some types of airplanes (Airbus A320, for example), because of the aerodynamic characteristics in the approach to stall, the stall warning threshold is often independent of Mach. On the A330 and other airplanes of its generation, the stall warning angle of attack is adjusted by Mach number.

The stall margin at cruise altitude/Mach is quite small. The stall warning is set to be sensitive, to give the pilot an indication that maneuvers must be made cautiously.

A complicating factor in activating the stall warning is calculating the Mach number in order to determine the stall angle of attack. If the airplane's sensors are compromised, as they were for much of AF447's ordeal, the stall warning will not accurately reflect the stall angle of attack for the current Mach number because it is not known.

On the A330, if no Mach is valid the warning threshold for values below Mach 0.3 is used. If the actual Mach number is .82 then the stall warning requires an angle of attack of over two times the correct one to activate, potentially resulting in no warning prior to the stall. However, in the AF447 case that was not a factor. There was never a time when the stall warning was inhibited by the stall warning threshold being incorrectly high. From the time of the initial stall at about 02:10:50, which was about 10 seconds before the peak altitude of 37,924 feet was reached, the actual angle of attack was always high enough to generate the stall warning whenever the AOA was considered valid (i.e., the airspeed was above 60 knots). The stall warning came on at about 6° AOA, and the stall buffet is recorded starting when the AOA passed through about 10° a few seconds later.

As long as the data from the angle of attack probes is considered valid, it will reference the stall warning from the AOA probe with the highest value. This may tend to produce the warning somewhat early due to gusts or turbulence, and as a result, would tend to be on only for short periods of time. Some refer to this as a "false warning," but it is a conservative approach to generating the warning. Studies show that most pilots, when presented with this scenario do not react strongly to the stall warning because while the triggering of the stall warning was noticed, it was unexpected and many crews tended to consider it as inconsistent with how they were handling the airplane, which would be that they were not making excessive inputs.[21]

A factor that may affect the ability to recover promptly from a stall is

---

21   AF447 Final Accident Report page 106

the effect of the application of thrust. With engines mounted below the center of gravity, like the A330 and many other large transports, an application of thrust induces a pitch-up moment. This is obviously contrary to the pitch down required to reduce the angle of attack and recover from the stall. If other pitch-down capabilities are compromised (e.g., aft CG, low elevator effectiveness from a nose-high stab trim setting), a high power setting may actually inhibit the ability to pitch the nose down and recover from the stall condition, or may at least slow the pitch down maneuver. This is not a consideration that was well taught until recently. At the time of the accident, the first step in response to a stall was the application of full power.

AF447 may have been in a position where reduction of thrust would have helped bring about an effective recovery. There are two points where nose down inputs were made, one at about 24,000 feet and the other around 9,000 feet. In each instance the pitch down command was followed by a pitch reduction and a decrease in the angle of attack. The pitch reduction resulted in a nose-down attitude of as low as of 8° below the horizon (which would look and feel quite steep), but the angle of attack only reduced from 40° to 35°, and therefore remained many times higher than the stall angle of attack. The airplane would have needed to pitch down significantly more to completely restore proper airflow over the wings, followed by a pitch up maneuver, being careful not to stall again in a high-g pull up.

Unfortunately, sufficient nose down inputs were not held long enough to complete the recovery. In fact, aggressive nose down inputs were never made for more than a few seconds, and when they were, they were followed with nose-up inputs by Bonin in the right seat. Even though the engines were at about climb power or greater for both events, the majority of the elevator's range of movement remained unused. This indicates to me that the ability to pitch down and reduce the angle of attack enough to recover remained a possibility. However, a lower power setting might have helped the nose pitch down faster. Correction of the full nose-up trim may also have been required to regain full pitch control.

How much altitude it would have taken to complete the recovery is anyone's guess, many thousands of feet for sure. Even the experts at Airbus declined to guess where the last point the airplane was recoverable from might be.

Since the accident, the FAA and the main aircraft manufacturers, including Airbus, ATR, Boeing, Bombardier and Embraer, have gotten together and issued a joint stall recovery technique that displaces the application of full power as the first step. The focus is now on using pitch to reduce the angle of attack, then followed by application of power when the airplane is under control again.

Flight Controls

No Airbus discussion, and no in-depth discussion of this accident is complete without covering the Airbus's fly-by-wire flight control laws. Almost immediately after the loss of reliable airspeed data, this A330's flight controls had degraded from Normal Law to Alternate Law. (The laws are explained later.) The aircraft's handling characteristics changed slightly and most in-flight protections were lost.

Fly by Wire Introduction

In a fly-by-wire control system, included on airplanes like the Airbus A320, A330, A340, A380, and Boeing 777 & 787, the pilot's inputs are provided to sophisticated flight control computers that then position the flight controls according to programming, called flight control laws.

Computers can be programmed to behave in any way desired, so engineers worked to program out characteristics that they deemed undesirable and programmed in behaviors that were favored instead. The latest jet fighters, bombers, and the space shuttle are all fly-by-wire, and it is said that many would be virtually uncontrollable were it not for the fly-by-wire system.

SideSticks

Airbus fly-by-wire aircraft use a sidestick controller and conventional rudder pedals for pilot control inputs. Stick-type controllers are no stranger to most pilots and are found in aircraft ranging from gliders, helicopters, and Piper Cubs to jet fighter aircraft and the Space Shuttle. On the Airbus, the stick controllers are positioned forward and outboard of each pilot's seat and are therefore called sidesticks.

Each sidestick is lightly spring loaded to its center detent. Each is equipped with a combination autopilot-disconnect/takeover push button (the red button in the photo above), and a push-to-talk trigger on the front side for communications. The two sidesticks are not mechanically linked, nor do they move unless the pilot moves them. Moving one, does not move the other. Except on the ground, the position of the sidesticks is not displayed.

It is difficult to see the other sidestick, and in flight there is no indication of its position to either pilot. If both sidesticks are moved at the same time, their inputs are summed. Full forward on one and full back on the other results in no pitch command, but that is contrary to how it should be flown. However, when both sidesticks are out of the center detent at the same time, a green light in front of each pilot flashes, and a synthetic voice calls out "DUAL INPUT." This "DUAL INPUT" call was heard on the AF447 cockpit voice recording during three separate time periods.

All pilots are taught that only one pilot should be flying at a time, and that is no exception with the sidesticks. In an Airbus that discipline is critical. The voice recorder transcript includes exchanges of that transfer of control, e.g., "I have the controls."

The takeover pushbutton is not meant to resolve a fight over who is flying the airplane. Its primary function is to override erroneous inputs due to mechanical or electrical malfunction. When a pilot's sidestick is being overridden due to the opposite takeover pushbutton, a red arrow illuminates on the glareshield in front of the pilot losing control, pointing to the pilot who has taken control. The last pilot to push the button gains control overriding opposite sidestick's inputs while it is held down. If held for more than 40 seconds, the opposite sidestick is locked out until its takeover pushbutton is pressed. The point is that simultaneous dual input is not only against procedure, but when it happens, both aural and visual indications alert the crew so that a dangerous or confusing situation can be avoided.

The sidestick design is not without its detractors, including those that believe their design to be a contributing factor to the accident.

While it is difficult to see the other pilot's sidestick position, there is rarely a reason to. The combined input is shown on the Primary Flight Display (PFD) only on the ground, intended for use in pre-takeoff flight control check. But again, the opposite sidestick can be assumed to be in neutral unless the green light is on and "DUAL INPUT" is being repeatedly announced.

When Captain Dubois returned to the cockpit, one minute and forty seconds after the autopilot disconnected, it is assumed he was positioned aft of the center pedestal, between the two pilots, or possibly sitting on the jumpseat in the same location. From that position, the sidesticks would have been blocked from view, unless he deliberately leaned forward to look.

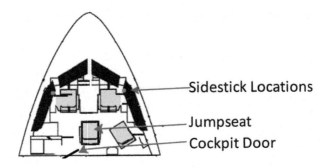

The evidence that the hidden sidestick position was an issue is that as they were descending through about 9,000 feet, Robert told Bonin to "climb, climb, climb, climb." When Bonin responded that he had "been at maxi nose up for a while," the captain responded with "no, no, no, don't climb," and Robert took the controls within a few seconds. One theory is that had there been a big control yoke in front of both pilots, and one was pulling back as the stall warning was going off, it would be readily apparent to everyone what was happening and it could have been corrected earlier. In fact, there are a few seconds before Bonin relinquished the controls that his sidestick was all the way back, Robert's was all the way forward, and no pitch change occurred. This obviously could not happen with mechanically linked controls.

Pilots transitioning from conventional flight control aircraft to the sidestick do so quite easily and naturally. Most will have flown some type of stick controlled aircraft in their career making it a natural transition. Even for those that have not, it is rarely an issue. However, the sidestick input is best flown with a gentle hand. Light fingertip pressure is often all that is needed to fly precisely. A firm grip and strong inputs are almost certain to result in over controlling the airplane. Constant displacement on the sidestick is almost never required, but that is exactly what the pilot flying aboard AF447 was doing as he was losing control of the airplane.

Flight Control Laws

In the past, flight controls were designed to meet two sets of criteria: they had to be "well harmonized" and had to meet the criteria for certification. With fly-by-wire, three possibilities have been added: improved safety by restricting maneuvers which could lead to a loss of control, reduced weight of the structure with the prohibition of some actions which may increase the loads, and finally improved comfort for the passengers.[22]

On the Airbus family, the flight control laws are similar, but not exactly the same between models A319/320/321, A330/A340, A380, and soon, the A350. Each enjoy the results of progress in design with their respective age, as well as differences due to the nature of the aircraft itself. The point being that the A320 flight control system, flight control laws and the transition between them are not the same as the A330. As a result, there are a number of posts, articles, and opinions based on A320 flight control system that do not apply correctly to the A330.

On the A330, the flight control laws are provided by five redundant computers: 3 Primary (also called PRIMs or FCPC [Flight Control Primary Computer]), and 2 Secondary (also called SECs or FCSC [Flight Control Secondary Computer]). The flight control computers control the two ailerons and seven spoilers on each wing, the two independent elevators, trimmable horizontal stabilizer, and the rudder, using hydraulic actuators powered by 3 independent hydraulic systems. (Flaps and slats are controlled by a separate computer.)

Each computer controls specific hydraulic actuators for the flight control surfaces. All of the flight control surfaces can be actuated by at least two hydraulic actuators (except spoilers which each have one and the rudder which has three) and each actuator on the inboard ailerons and elevators can be driven by either of two computers. Suffice it to say there is a lot of redundancy built into the system that even with multiple hydraulic and flight control computer failures, control of the airplane can be maintained, although handling may be degraded.

---

22   Airbus "Safety First" Development of A380 Flight Controls part 1

There are four basic levels of flight control laws:

- Normal Law
- Alternate Law (with two versions: Alternate 1 and Alternate 2)
- Direct Law
- Backup Control

Airbus refers to the flight control laws other than Normal Law as reconfiguration laws.

Normal Law is the flight control law normally in effect unless there are multiple failures. Normal Law allows the airplane to handle consistently throughout the flight envelope with automatic trim. For each movement of the sidestick, instead of commanding a specific amount of flight control surface deflection, Normal Law commands a performance. So the same sidestick input consistently results in the same aircraft handling response. The amount of flight control surface deflection required to provide that performance will vary with airspeed and other conditions. While the control deflection can be seen on the flight control display, it is not normally monitored except for a pre-takeoff control check. Normal Law also provides the highest degree of protections to prevent the airplane from leaving the normal operating envelope. Protections are provided for high and low speed (including stall protection), bank and pitch angles, and g load. Though not usually listed as a protection, roll rate is also limited by the design.

In the roll axis, sidestick deflection signals a rate-of-roll demand. This means that for a given amount of sidestick deflection left or right, the pilot commands a given roll rate, with a maximum of 15° per second. The center position commands a zero roll rate, or in other words, maintain the current bank angle.

In pitch, Normal Law provides a g-load/pitch-rate demand. This means that for a given amount of sidestick deflection forward or aft, the pilot commands a consistent pitch response. At higher speeds this is best expressed in the g-force as a result of the pitch maneuver, at other times the pitch rate is a better measure. The center position commands 1 g, or unaccelerated flight (which could be in a climb, level, or descent). The result is the flight path is maintained. If flaps are extended or retracted the airplane will automatically adjust the pitch in order to maintain the same flight path. In normal operation this reduces the workload of hand flying the airplane. The stab trim is set automatically because the flight control system holds the airplane as commanded whether it is in trim or not. In Normal and Alternate laws, the pilot does not receive feedback on the trim status, nor does he need any.

Normal Law provides two key low-speed reference points: Alpha Protect (commonly, Alpha Prot) and Alpha Max. As the name Alpha implies, a term meaning angle of attack, even though they are represented on the airspeed indicator, they are actually referenced to angle of attack.

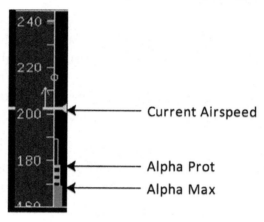

Airspeed Indicator

When slowing, as the angle of attack reaches Alpha Prot the sidestick transforms from a g-load demand to an angle-of-attack-demand input.

Alpha Max is an angle of attack just below stall, that is the maximum angle of attack allowed by the low-speed protections.

The airspeed at which Alpha Prot occurs is lower than normal operating speeds but higher than the stall speed. When operating between Alpha Prot and Alpha Max, the center/neutral sidestick position commands Alpha Prot, and full back commands Alpha Max. Therefore, in Normal Law, the airplane will pitch down on its own if the angle of attack increases to Alpha-Prot, but the pilot retains the authority to command a higher angle of attack. Once the angle of attack reaches Alpha Max, the flight control laws will not allow the angle of attack to increase further and will control the pitch to keep the AOA at or below Alpha Max. Because of this, the pilot can command a maximum performance maneuver by holding the sidestick all the way back.

For Air France 447, when the transition to Alternate Law was made, these angle of attack limits no longer functioned.

A Different Relationship

In an airplane with conventional flight controls the resultant roll or pitch rate would more directly correlate with the force applied to the control wheel, and not the amount of deflection required. At higher speeds less control deflection is required to achieve the desired performance, and the airflow over the control surfaces makes the controls correspondingly stiffer. At low speeds greater control deflection is required and the controls feel "sloppy."

On the fly-by-wire system, the sidesticks do not provide tactile feedback of flight control force. Sidestick deflection correlates to the desired performance. The system determines how much to move the actual controls surfaces to satisfy the demand. Therefore, airplane handling and response is consistent throughout the flight envelope.

The Airbus pilot must occasionally remind himself of this different relationship. I have told many students "you are telling it what to do, not how to do it." Airbus pilots will have trouble if they forget this principle. One common instance is during approach with turbulence. Most pilots of conventionally controlled airplanes are used to instantly responding with a wind gust that tips a wing with a corresponding lateral control input. With the sidestick in neutral, an Airbus will attempt to maintain a zero roll rate on its own, and will automatically input a roll command in response to the gust. Pilots who react to each bump and gust end up creating their own turbulence by wagging the sidestick back and forth faster than the airplane can respond. With each movement of the sidestick, the pilot is asking for a different performance (roll left, roll right), and it takes some time for this to all happen. It is not difficult to get into a situation where the inexperienced Airbus pilot is reacting to his previous sidestick input.

Despite how it may sound, the transition to this different flight control/ performance relationship is quite easy. Pilots do not normally think of how much control deflection they need to achieve a given pitch or roll rate, but will use as much as required with the airplane's response as a cue. Likewise with the sidestick, the pilot inputs as much control input as necessary to achieve the desired performance and do not give it a second thought.

Another situation where this different relationship becomes significant is during crosswind landings. During the approach the airplane is crabbed into the wind, flying somewhat sideways to the runway. It is a normal procedure during the pre-touchdown stage of a crosswind landing to use the rudder to align the airplane with the runway so that the wheels touchdown in line with their axis of rotation. When the airplane is aligned with the runway, drift is controlled with the input of a slight bank angle.

A properly input bank angle balances out the effect of a crosswind. To maintain this balance rudder and opposite aileron must both be deflected. In a conventional airplane, this is done be holding the rudder and the control wheel both deflected in opposite directions, referred to as a cross-control input. But on Airbus fly-by-wire aircraft, the sidestick commands rate of roll and not aileron deflection. Therefore, if the sidestick was held as in a conventionally controlled airplane, the airplane would continue to increase its bank angle as long as the sidestick was held deflected.

The Airbus pilot must learn to use the sidestick only to establish the bank angle, and then return it to neutral in order to maintain the bank angle. This is not particularly difficult, but it does require an conscious understanding of what the sidestick is commanding.

As an interesting contrast to the Airbus fly-by-wire design, the Boeing 777 (also a fly-by-wire airplane) directly commands aileron deflection for roll so that airplane mimics one that is conventionally controlled.

The B-787 on the other hand, uses a rate-of-roll demand for lateral inputs, similar to Airbus aircraft. But the engineers also designed in a roll response to rudder pedal input so that in a cross control situation the pilot inputs can be conventional. The simultaneous control wheel and rudder pedal commanded roll rates cancel each other out. This provides the excellent handling characteristics of a roll-rate demand with the crosswind handling that pilots are used to.

As mentioned earlier, Normal Law in addition to providing well behaved and consistent handling characteristics, also provides the highest level of protections. These protections are designed to prevent loss of control and exceeding the normal operating parameters. Protections are provided for g load, pitch and roll attitudes, speed, and angle of attack.

Some naysayers describe the protections as the pilot wanting something and the computers deciding if they will allow it, implying that the pilot always knows better and should always be obeyed. The pilot commands a performance not a control command. There is no reasonable scenario where a transport category airplane should be rolled, looped, stalled or significantly oversped. There is however, an accident history where these parameters were inadvertently exceeded ending in disaster. The protections are there for a good reason.

In roll, the sidestick commands a rate up to 15° per second, which is quite fast. In airline operations bank angles rarely exceed 30°, and Normal Law reflects that. At bank angles up to 33° if the stick is returned to neutral, the airplane will maintain that bank angle all day long. For bank angles beyond 33° lateral sidestick deflection must be held in, as these bank angles are allowed, but unusual. If the sidestick is released back to neutral the airplane will automatically reduce the bank to 33°. This is known as a "spiral stability." At 67° of bank, full left or right sidestick deflection must be held to maintain this unusual bank angle. This bank angle also correlates to 2.5g's in level flight, the positive g-load limit.

In pitch, Normal Law limits pitch attitude to 30° nose up and 15° nose down. These would be extremes in any airline operation.

High speed protection will pitch the airplane up when the maximum speed is exceeded to slow it down and prevent damage to the airframe. However, the pilot can command a transient of about 20 knots beyond the upper limit with forward stick input.

Low speed protection references the angle of attack and will automatically pitch the airplane down as necessary to protect from stall. It establishes a neutral point at Alpha-Prot. To go beyond that (lower speed, higher angle of attack) requires the pilot to pull back on the sidestick.

These protections allow the Airbus pilot to ask for the maximum performance by simply moving the control to the limit. For example, in a terrain avoidance maneuver (e.g., mountain ahead) a maximum performance climb is required, but the pilot must not risk stalling or over-stressing the airplane. In a conventionally controlled airplane, this is up to the pilot to manage. There is no g-meter available to show the relationship to the g limit, and the pilot must attempt to operate near the stall warning point in order to achieve the maximum lift from the wings. It is difficult to do this in a precise manner. Some Boeing airplanes display an angle-of-attack based pitch limit indicator (PLI) on the attitude indicator for assistance. The Airbus fly-by-wire system allows the pilot to pull back on the sidestick all the way to achieve maximum performance without risk of stall or exceeding the g limit. The full back sidestick does not command full up elevator, but up to 2.5 g's (or the AOA limit)—a maximum performance pull up.

Studies show that when the pilot can go directly and confidently to the maximum performance input, the airplane's flight path is also significantly better in terms of terrain clearance.

When the pitch attitude approaches 30° nose up the pitch attitude protection becomes active to prevent an excessively nose high attitude, which could quickly result in a dangerously slow airspeed (there is not enough power to sustain a climb at that attitude). As the airspeed slows and the angle of attack increases to alpha-protect, the protections will automatically pitch the airplane down to maintain a safe margin above stall. At this point, pulling back on the sidestick can command an even higher angle of attack, to achieve a higher degree of lift from the wing, close to the stall point. Full back stick commands the maximum angle of attack (Alpha Max), slightly less than the stall angle of attack, for the highest coefficient of lift from the wing. The stall warning is not necessary in Normal Law.

A windshear recovery uses the same principles, and allows the pilot to ask for maximum performance when achieving what is critical to survival. In a severe windshear scenario, the sidestick can be held full back if required. The airplane will respond with changing pitch attitudes in order to provide maximum performance, a feat that is difficult at best to do manually.

The airplane does not disregard what the pilot has instructed it to do with a full back sidestick input or other maximum control inputs. This is a matter of interpretation of what the pilot wants—full up elevator or maximum escape performance.

The simplicity with which Normal Law can keep the airplane within the normal operating range and provide maximum recovery performance may have been what the pilot flying on AF447 remembered when things went wrong and the flight control laws degraded to Alternate Law. Full power and pull back is an effective escape maneuver for emergency terrain avoidance and windshear recovery, and also provides stall protection. However, only in Normal Law and only at low altitude when lots of extra power is available.

Alternate Law

When failures no longer make it possible to carry out Normal Law, other reconfiguration laws take effect. The failures could be failures in the physical flight control systems, hydraulics, computers, or the information needed to carry out the laws themselves.

Some of that information comes from the three Air Data Reference units (ADR) which are combined with the three Inertial Reference units (IR) making up the Air Data Inertial Reference System (ADIRS). For Normal Law to operate, requires two of the three air data sources to agree so that there is reasonable assurance that the data is reliable.

The next step below Normal Law is Alternate Law.

Alternate Law has two basic versions, depending on what has failed: Alternate 1 and Alternate 2.

In either case, an ECAM message displays "ALTN LAW (PROT LOST)" (Alternate Law, protections lost), and a second line states that the speed should be limited to 330 kts/ .82 Mach (slightly less than the Normal Law limitations). Additionally amber X's replace the green equal signs that are displayed at the pitch and roll limits when Normal Law is active.

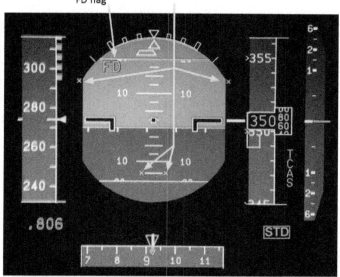

Green = signs replaced by amber XX's in Alternate law
FD flag

The main difference between the two levels of Alternate Law is in the roll portion of the law. In Alternate 1, the roll command remains rate-of-roll, like Normal Law. Bank angle protection (67°) remains in place, but is lost in case of triple ADR failure or ADR disagree.

In Alternate 2 the roll command is a direct stick-to-control command with no protections or stabilities. A few spoilers are inhibited to keep the potential roll rates from being excessive, and the gains on the flight controls are set according to the flap/slat position.[23] Alternate 2 is activated with an ADR disagree or dual ADR or IR fault as well as with some other multiple failures of the flight control system.

At low altitude, the two sub-modes do not really handle that differently, and pilots often have a hard time telling them apart, though Alternate 2 is more sensitive in roll. At high altitude, the same control deflection can result in higher roll rates due to less aerodynamic damping, usually a minor effect. The long fuel-filled wing and the weight of the engines also add a rolling inertia component. In Normal and Alternate 1 laws, since the sidestick commands the rate of roll, those effects are automatically compensated for. However, in Alternate 2 and Direct laws, the sidestick commands the control surfaces directly, so the controls must be used with care to prevent over controlling, and with the realization that once the wing is in motion, it won't stop instantly just because the control is centered. The difficulty with roll control may have directed the flying pilot's attention away from the pitch control.

Immediately after the autopilot disconnected, the airplane rolled into an 8° right bank in about 2 seconds due to external forces. First Officer Bonin corrected with up to ½ left sidestick input. Within the same two seconds the airplane rolled 14° left to a 6° left bank.

As the airplane rolled through wings level to the left the sidestick was moved about half way to the right. The lateral sidestick displacement and the airplane's bank angle became exactly out of phase (peak bank angle in one direction with peak control input in the other), and the airplane rolled back to the right. The second and third lateral inputs reached the full stick input to the left and ¾ to the right.

---

23   This is similar to the normal operation of many conventionally controlled transport airplanes, which will lockout or limit some surfaces with flaps or slats extended.

For 30 seconds he struggled to get the bank angle under control. The bank angle was never excessive, the maximum was only 11°. But the dynamics of the roll response made it difficult to control, and may have added to a lack of attention in the vertical axis. For halfway through his efforts to control the bank angle, the vertical speed reached 6,900 feet per minute and First Officer Robert called out, "Watch your speed, watch your speed."

Bonin started to reduce the pitch attitude, "Okay okay, okay I'm going back down," he said, as he struggled to control both pitch and roll.

Precious airspeed was lost during this time. It was only after the roll was back under control that First Officer Robert offered the advice, "Above all try to touch the lateral controls as little as possible." But by then, the stall warning had started to sound and loss of control was only seconds away.

In determining the active flight control law, the flight control computers monitor the input from the various sources. When only two sources agree the third value gets voted out. For the purpose of the flight control system, when one of the three airspeed sources deviates too much from the other two it is automatically rejected by the PRIMs and the voted value then becomes the average of the two remaining airspeeds. In this scenario, Normal Law continues to function.

The remaining airspeed values are then monitored both individually and collectively. If the difference between the two remaining values becomes too great, the PRIMs reject them both and the control law reconfigures to Alternate 2.

If voted value falls by more than 30 knots in one second, then that will also trigger a reconfiguration to Alternate 2 Law. In the case of AF447, the indicated airspeed fell from 274 to 52 knots within 3 seconds (an average drop of 74 knots/second) and as a result, Normal Law degraded to Alternate 2.

In both Alternate 1 and Alternate 2 the pitch law remains the same as in Normal Law. That is, g-load demand with maneuver (maximum g load) protection. The "hard" speed protections are lost. If there is enough data available, the hard protections are replaced by low and high speed "stabilities."

Stabilities function similar to a conventionally controlled airplane that is out of trim. With the sidestick in neutral, if the airspeed approaches a limit, the airplane wants to pitch down or pitch up to return to the trimmed airspeed. Without the stabilities the unaltered g-load demand control system will provide no resistance to going dangerously fast or slow. The stabilities will gently pitch the airplane down or up if the sidestick is near neutral. The pilot can override the stabilities by holding the sidestick forward or back. The force required is the same as moving the sidestick at any other time, and as a result the effect is somewhat subtle.

Low speed stability is activated by reference to indicated airspeed, not angle of attack. It is active from 5 to 10 knots above stall speed. When low speed stability is active, automatic stabilizer trim stops and the pitch law changes to Direct Law. This restores the airplane's natural stability, and it will tend to pitch down.

If the aircraft weight data, flap position data, or a dual or triple air data loss or disagreement occurs, the low speed stabilities cannot function. The g-load pitch law remains in effect and automatic trim continues to operate. This was the case with AF447.

Alternate Law requires awareness as no computerized protections or aerodynamic pitch down forces will assist in maintaining flight within the normal operating envelope. This is why the ECAM says "Alternate Law, protections lost." In the Flight Crew Training Manual, Airbus states, "Outside the normal flight envelope, the PF must take appropriate preventive actions to avoid losing control, and/or avoid high speed excursions. These actions are the same as those that would be applied in any case of a non-protected aircraft (e.g., in case of stall warning: add thrust, reduce pitch, check speedbrakes retracted)." However, the speed stabilities are not lost in conventional aircraft.

AF447 lost airspeed indications at some points while the values disagreed at others, therefore the low speed stabilities were not available due to both reasons.

The final report states:

> Specifically, the approach to stall on a classic airplane is always associated with a more or less pronounced nose-up input. This is not the case on the A330 in alternate law. The specific consequence is that in this control law the airplane, placed in a configuration where the thrust is not sufficient to maintain speed on the flight path, would end up by stalling without any inputs on the sidestick. It appears that this absence of positive static stability could have contributed to the PF not identifying the approach to stall.

If the PF had simply pointed the nose of the airplane up and made no more pitch inputs, the outcome might have been much the same. However, Bonin *did* make nose up inputs. His inability to conclude that the airplane would quickly run out of energy while making these inputs and that a stall was a genuine threat is baffling.

Abnormal Attitude Law

Some have speculated that the particulars of Alternate Law worked contrary to the recovery, and if the pilots had more authority a recovery may have been easier. Abnormal Attitude Law is an automatically engaged law designed to give the pilots additional authority in rare occasions, such as extreme windshear or structural damage. If the airplane exceeds the following parameters, Abnormal Attitude Law becomes active:

- Pitch attitude > 50° nose up or 30° nose down
- Bank angle > 125°
- Angle of attack > 30° or < -10°
- Speed > 440 kt or < 60 kt
- Mach > 0.96 or < 0.1

Unlike Alternate 2 Law where some spoilers are disabled and the flight control gains are set according to flap position, Abnormal Attitude Law provides a full-authority direct law in roll. This provides the pilot the highest capacity to recover from unforeseen circumstances.

In the pitch axis, Abnormal Attitude Law provides Alternate Law pitch handling with no protections except g load. Auto trim is also disabled.

When the recovery is complete, the flight control law reverts to Alternate 2 Law and remains there for the rest of the flight.

Due to the rejection of the speed and angle of attack data by the primary flight control computers on AF447, the Abnormal Attitude Law could only have been triggered by a pitch or bank angle exceedance, but neither of those conditions were ever met.

While it may have been helpful if the pitch trim was disabled at some point to aid in recovery, by the time the angle of attack reached 30°, the stabilizer was already close to full nose up trim due to the prolonged application of pitch-up commands by the pilot. After the stall at 38,000 feet, the pilots were not fully using the authority they already had to make the recovery. Therefore, even if Abnormal Attitude Law had engaged, it most likely would not have made any difference. Also, in consideration of the difficult time that First Officer Bonin had controlling the roll axis of the airplane with the dampened roll response of Alternate 2 Law, given the same control inputs, the full roll authority of Abnormal Attitude Law may well have resulted in more extreme roll excursions and further loss of control.

Flight Directors

The flight director on the A330 consists of a pitch and a roll command bar displayed on the attitude portion of the Primary Flight Display (PFD). The flight directors provide guidance for following the selected pitch and roll modes by displacing the command bar from the center position. Each command bar operates separately to instruct the pilot to make a pitch or roll input.

Flight directors allow the pilot to hand fly the airplane very precisely by responding to even small displacements of the command bars. This relieves the pilot of the task of scanning the instruments for deviations from the desired path and speed, calculating any needed correction, making an attitude adjustment to initiate the correction, monitoring the correction, resuming an attitude to maintain the desired path, and repeating every few seconds. In this way, flight directors allow for reduced mental workload and increased accuracy when hand flying.

The autopilot and the flight director both operate in the same mode when either is on, with the guidance selected by the pilot and computed by the Flight Management Guidance and Envelope Computer (FMGEC). The selected modes for the autopilot and/or flight director are displayed at the top of the PFD in an area referred to as the Flight Mode Annunciator (FMA). The FMA has separate columns for autothrust, pitch, roll, and autopilot/flight director/autothrust status. Engaged modes are displayed in green, and armed modes in blue. Newly engaged modes are surrounded by a white box.

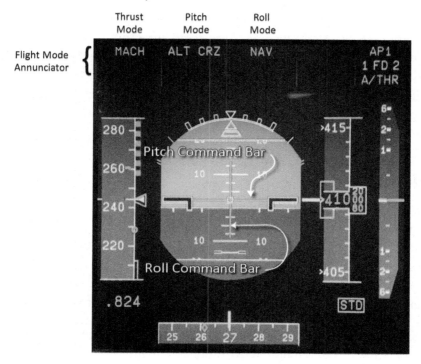

The flight directors provide guidance from shortly after takeoff to landing. They can provide guidance for all normal operations and even low altitude windshear recovery, but not for traffic or terrain avoidance or stall recovery.

The flight directors are extremely reliable. Unfortunately, it is easy to fall into the trap of following the flight directors so intently that the actual instrument indications are ignored.

They will automatically disappear when the data upon which their commands are based is not agreed upon by two out of three sources, or when abnormal pitch or bank angles are reached. They will change modes or disappear if the speed becomes excessively high or low, with the new mode annunciated on the FMA. If they reengage after disappearing they will return in the vertical speed/heading mode at the vertical speed and heading that exists at the time. However, they do not automatically reengage in all situations.

In the case of Air France 447, the flight directors disappeared when the airspeed sources no longer agreed with each other and the autopilot disconnected. They reappeared several times during the subsequent climb, but they would not have been providing appropriate guidance to recover back to level flight. What is not known is if the pilots attempted to follow them.

Flight Path Vector

The A330 has an indication known as the Flight Path Vector (FPV). It is an optional display that can be used at any time. The flight path vector shows the actual flight path of the airplane both vertically and horizontally, independent of the pitch attitude. The FPV is derived from a combination of inertial data and altitude data. The values are derived from the barometric altimeter data, even if that is erroneous.

In the photo below the FPV is the green symbol on the horizon line. Notice that the airplane's pitch attitude is actually about 9.5° up, but the FPV indicates that the flight path of the airplane is on the horizon, or level flight. If the airplane were descending, the FPV would be below the horizon an amount that corresponded with the descent angle.

If a crosswind exists, the FPV is displaced to either side of center to illustrate the actual direction of movement, despite the heading. The angle between the center of the display and the FPV represents the drift angle.

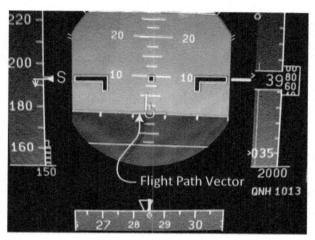

Flight Path Vector

The crew of AF447 did not display the FPV during this flight. But an ACARS maintenance message was sent when the symbol was not available due a loss of data (calibrated airspeed below 60 knots), so I mention it here. The first interim report of the accident incorrectly stated that the error message indicated that the FPV was selected and unavailable. It was later corrected to clarify that the FPV did not need to be selected to generate the error message.

The display of the FPV may have been useful in maintaining level flight shortly after the autopilot disconnected. It might have also been useful to confirm that the airplane was in fact descending during the time when they appear to have been seriously doubting their altimeter indications.

When the FPV is displayed and the flight directors are on, the flight directors are presented as Flight Path Directors, where the pilots flies the FPV symbol to match the flight path director commands. Like the cross-bar flight directors, they provide no stall recovery guidance.

Once the airplane started to descend, the FPV would have been well below the horizon line, potentially further leading the pilot to pull back to correct the flight path. It would have eventually gone off the bottom of the scale altogether.

It is hard to say that the attempted use of the flight path vector could have made the situation worse, for the final outcome could not have been much worse than it already was. However, it might have aided the pilot flying in maintaining altitude early on if he did not know what pitch attitude to fly to maintain level flight once the autopilot, flight director, and airspeed were unavailable.

ECAM

System displays, alerts, and corrective actions are displayed on the ECAM (Electronic Centralized Aircraft Monitor (pronounced ē-cam). The ECAM consists of the two center screens on the forward instrument panel.

The upper screen or Engine/Warning Display (E/WD) displays the primary engine instruments, slat/flap positions, total fuel, and warning, caution, and advisory messages.

The lower screen displays the status of the various aircraft systems and takes the place of numerous dials and gauges in earlier generation aircraft. It also displays a STATUS page where a summary of inoperative components, preparations for landing, and other in-flight reminders are displayed.

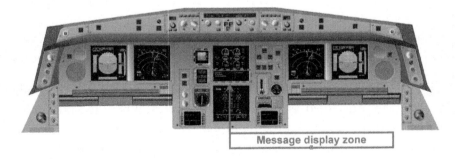

Message display zone

When there is a system malfunction, the title of the malfunction is displayed along with a checklist of actions to stabilize or correct the situation. Crews use the messages and checklists displayed on the ECAM to address each one in an orderly manner. Messages are prioritized into warnings, cautions, and advisory messages, with the most important messages, the warnings always displayed first.

Each level of message, and some specific faults, also have an associated aural annunciation. An autopilot disconnect invokes a repeating "cavalry charge." Other warnings sound a continuous repetitive chime (ding ding ding ...), cautions a single chime (ding), and advisories have no sound.

The stall warning consists of a cricket sound and the words "STALL STALL" spoken by a synthetic voice. The red master warning light in front of each pilot is also illuminated.

A "C-chord" tone sounds in association with altitude. It is intended as an altitude awareness reminder. It sounds for 1.5 seconds when approaching a selected altitude if the autopilot is off, and sounds continuously when deviating more than 200 feet from the selected altitude. The continuous C-chord can be silenced by pushing the Master Warning light/switch on the forward glareshield. This C-chord is an indication of an unusual situation (deviation from the assigned altitude), and it is not normal for it to sound, or to cancel it. On AF447, the C-chord first sounded within eight seconds of the autopilot disconnecting and remained on for almost the entire rest of the flight. It was only silent as they approached and descended through their original altitude of FL350 and when it was overridden by a higher priority audio alert such as the stall warning.

When a malfunction occurs, the acting pilot in command should assign duties (e.g., "You fly the airplane and take the radios, I'll work the ECAM.") Crews are trained and expected to handle each message in order starting at the top warning message and complete the associated steps in a methodical manner.

Some messages will clear themselves when the condition no longer applies or the step is completed, but not all. The ECAM system also includes a CLEAR key on the control panel that allows the pilot to clear messages so that additional messages can be read on the limited screen space, or to progress through the ECAM procedure.

Once the messages and associated checklists have been completed or cleared, the ECAM system will display the pages of individual aircraft systems that have been affected by the non-normal conditions. For example, if a generator failed, after the generator fail message and the steps to attempt to reset or turn off the generator, the electrical system schematic will be displayed showing the failed generator and the electrical system's reconfiguration. The clear key allows movement to the next affected system.

After the affected systems are displayed, the STATUS page is displayed. The status page shows a list of inoperative items, reminders, and additional steps in preparation for landing.

Some malfunctions have memory items because action is required right away and the malfunction may not be automatically detected and displayed on the ECAM. In cases where the ECAM does not, or cannot, detect the anomaly, crews should call for the appropriate procedure from the paper version in the Quick Reference Handbook (QRH). This is the case in the instance of unreliable airspeed. There was no ECAM message for loss of airspeed. A memory item and paper checklist procedure applied.

Crews are not expected or trained to make up procedures and actions. However, a level of systems knowledge is expected that would allow them to understand the procedure steps and make appropriate decisions.

In any case, maintaining aircraft control is always the first order of business. In the AF447 accident it is clear that the crew failed to maintain control of the airplane as the first priority, suffered a loss of ECAM discipline, and made a venture into making up corrective actions.

Illustrated below is the initial ECAM indication that appeared within about 5 seconds after the autopilot disconnected. Each message starts with the affected system, the associated malfunction, and then corrective actions, if available.

```
ECAM    02:10:08

AUTO FLT AP OFF
F/CTL ALTN LAW
       (PROT LOST)
-MAX SPEED.......330/.82
AUTO FLT
REAC W/S DET FAULT
```

The first line in red is a warning level annunciation for the autopilot disconnection. The underlined "AUTO FLT" indicates the affected system is the autoflight system. AP OFF indicates that the autopilot is now off by other than pilot selection. There are no corrective actions associated with this message—the crew must now hand fly the airplane.

The system does not necessarily make the cause of a failure clear. When the internal crosschecks of the airspeed parameters found a disagreement and caused the autoflight systems to shut off, it did not annunciate that there was an airspeed discrepancy. It only alerted the pilots that the autoflight systems had been turned off. One of the recommendations of the accident report is that when specific monitoring is triggered, the crew be alerted to facilitate comprehension of the situation. Essentially, "airspeed discrepancy: autopilot is off" instead of the current system which amounts to, "autopilot is off, see if you can figure out why."

The next message was a caution level message relating to the flight control system, indicating that the airplane's active flight control law had changed to Alternate Law, followed by a reminder that the protections provided by Normal Law are now lost, and that the crew should not exceed 330 knots or Mach .82. This is a slight reduction from the normal maximum speed of 330 kts/Mach .86 due to the loss of the protection. The MAX SPEED step is always displayed with the Alternate Law annunciation and should have been familiar to the crew from training. The minimum speed remains unchanged. The report speculates that because only a maximum speed is shown and not a minimum speed, that "this could lead crews to suppose that the main risk is overspeed. In the absence of any reliable speed indication, this might lead to a protective nose-up input that is more or less instinctive."[24] I do not think this is the case, as the maximum speeds were not read out loud by First Officer Robert when he was performing the ECAM steps.

The third message, also autoflight related, indicates that the reactive windshear detection was rendered inoperative. That system only works below 1,200 feet above ground and requires a reliable airspeed indication. There are no steps associated with this item, and it would not have applied at their altitude anyway.

Shortly after the autopilot disconnected, the autothrust disconnected and its message appeared above the Alternate Law annunciation.

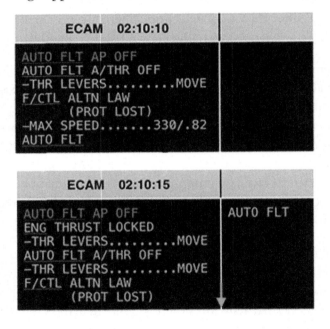

There were two messages associated with autothrust: <u>AUTO FLT</u> A/ THR OFF, and <u>ENG</u> THRUST LOCKED. The first message indicates that the autothrust has disconnected due to a fault, and the second that the engine speed is frozen at its last setting. Both include the corrective action, THRUST LEVERS ... MOVE, indicating that the pilot needs to take control of the thrust levers.

---

24   AF447 Final Accident Report page 174

On the ECAM display the THRUST LOCKED message appears above the autothrust-off message, and cycles on and briefly off every five seconds until the thrust levers are moved or the disconnect button is pushed. Each time it reappears a chime sounds, "ding!" to get the pilot's attention, insisting that the thrust levers be taken over manually.

At 02:10:16, 11 seconds after the autopilot disconnected, Robert said, "we've lost the speeds so …" He then read from the ECAM, "engine thrust A T H R engine lever thrust." His reading of the ECAM was imprecise. This is not due to a transcript translation error as he spoke in English.

Bonin questioned the reading, "Engine lever?"

At 02:10:22 Robert read, "Alternate Law protections lost." This was a major point that should have been made clear to the pilot flying. It indicates that the airplane will handle slightly differently, and that care must be taken to avoid exceeding the limits of the flight envelope.

At 02:10:23 instead of moving the thrust levers, the autothrust disconnect button was pushed before the THRUST LOCKED message chimed again, and because the thrust levers were in the climb detent, the thrust began to increase to climb thrust.

This is as far as they got in following the ECAM procedure.

The images above illustrate the display of the ECAM if no messages were cleared. The illustration below, shows all the faults and messages that would have been displayed in turn, had the clear function been used as intended. We do not know the extent to which the clear function was used, but because the transcript contains no more items read from the ECAM, it is reasonable to conclude that the ECAM was abandoned at that time.

The Theoretical Symptoms column lists the aural and warning light displays associated with each item:

MW: Master Warning Light (a red general purpose awareness light in front of each pilot)

MC: Master Caution Light (an amber general purpose awareness light in front of each pilot)

SC: Single Chime

Title	Theoretical symptoms	Time	Display Time
AUTO FLT AP OFF	cavalry charge + MW	02:10:05	02:10:05
AUTO FLT REAC W/S DET FAULT	SC + MC	02:10:06	02:10:07
F/CTL ALTN LAW (PROT LOST) ─MAX SPEED.......330/.82	SC + MC	02:10:06	02:10:08
AUTO FLT A/THR OFF ─THR LEVERS.........MOVE	SC + MC	02:10:08	02:10:10
ENG THRUST LOCKED ─THR LEVERS.........MOVE	SC + MC	02:10:08	02:10:15
NAV TCAS FAULT	SC + MC	02:10:xx	02:10:xx
F/CTL RUD TRV LIM FAULT RUD WITH CARE ABV 160 KT	SC + MC	02:10:18	02:10:19
NAV ADR DISAGREE ─AIR SPD.........X CHECK •IF NO SPD DISAGREE ─AOA DISCREPANCY •IF SPD DISAGREE ─ADR CHECK PROC..APPLY	SC + MC	02:12:xx	02:12:xx
F/CTL PRIM 1 FAULT	SC + MC	02:13:37	02:13:39
F/CTL SEC 1 FAULT	SC + MC	02:13:39	02:13:41

At 02:10:39 climbing through 37,000 feet First Officer Robert switched the source of the right side instruments to the #3 source for air data and attitude/heading, saying: "I'll put you in A-T-T." There is no ECAM step directing this, but if he doubted the accuracy of the instrument readings it is not an unreasonable thing to do.

The NAV ADR DISAGREE message at 02:12 indicated a disagreement between airspeed sources and did not annunciate until two minutes or more after the pitot clogging started. This may indicate that the left and right airspeed displays agreed up until that point, even if they were wrong. Since the right side display is not recorded, it is not possible to be sure. This message indicates that the primary flight control computer has rejected an air data reference (ADR), and then identified an inconsistency ("disagree") between the two remaining ADRs on one of the monitored parameters (i.e., airspeed). This condition left the system with no known trustworthy reference for the airspeed.

At 02:12:15 the selectors were positioned to place the left side instruments on the #3 source, immediately followed by First Officer Bonin saying "There you are." However, Bonin was the only person making control inputs at this time, so it is not clear who moved the selectors. It is clear why the air data source would be selected, but not why the attitude source was.

There were no comments made about unreliable attitude indications, though the captain did refer to the standby horizon at 02:12:23 while approaching 24,000 feet, "The wings to flat horizon, the standby horizon." (The standby horizon has independent sensors and is not connected to the three inertial reference systems or the ATT/HDG switch.) At 02:13:32 passing 10,000 feet the air data selector is placed back in the NORM position.

Seconds before the air data selector was positioned back to NORM, First Officer Robert told the captain, "Try to find what you can do with your controls up there, the primaries and so on." Despite the captain's remark that "It won't do anything" (he was correct), the final ECAM messages PRIM 1 FAULT and SEC 1 FAULT indicate that at 02:13:37 and :39 they were selected off—and presumably back on—in a reset attempt. This reset step is not in the procedure and is not a method for restoring Normal Law. It was a made-up corrective action.

Autothrust

The Airbus thrust lever design differs from that used on Boeing and most other aircraft that have autothrust/auto-throttles. The difference has led to some misstatements in articles concerning the meaning of the thrust lever positions, especially the term "TOGA."

Most other manufacturers use a motor driven servo to move the thrust levers to reflect the autothrust command to the engines. This is commonly called *autothrottle* as the system moves the throttles/thrust levers. This design allows for pilot awareness of engine activity, as he can see and feel the thrust levers move, and the pilot can change their position if the auto throttle system is not doing exactly what is desired. This design requires other switches to signal a desired change in mode, such as telling the autothrust system to select takeoff thrust, reduce to climb thrust, and to advance to and maintain power for a go-around. Proper settings for climb power, maximum continuous power, and full power are determined by setting the power according to the engine instruments.

On Airbus aircraft, when the autothrust is off, the pilot manually controls the thrust in a conventional manner, that is, engine speed correlates with thrust lever position.

The thrust levers have tactile detents at the climb power, maximum continuous power, and full forward stop which is the Take-Off/Go-Around position (TOGA). When the autothrust is on, and the thrust levers are between idle and the climb detent (known as the active range), the autothrust has the authority to control the thrust within that range. The lowest allowable thrust being idle (as used in descents) and the highest is the actual position of the thrust lever. The thrust levers are normally in the climb detent, but could be positioned to a lower setting to limit thrust, though it is rarely done. When the thrust levers are positioned out of this active range, i.e., moved above the climb detent, the thrust lever directly controls the engine speed, thus always allowing the pilot to gain control and add thrust by simply pushing the thrust levers forward.

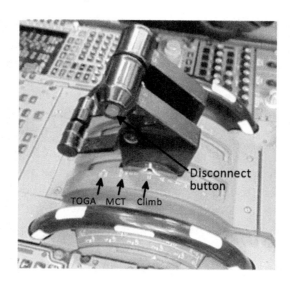

The design incorporates the selection of the various thrust modes simply by positioning the thrust lever itself, eliminating the need for other switches or selections in the flight management computer. In this system, the thrust levers are not back driven, saving the weight and complexity of the servo mechanism.

The thrust levers are normally placed in the climb (CLB) detent from shortly after takeoff until shortly before touchdown. So, it is a normal situation for the actual engine thrust to be something lower than the current position of the thrust levers. When the autothrust disconnects due to a failure, the actual engine thrust remains at its previous setting instead of suddenly matching up with the current thrust lever position. This mode is called "thrust lock". Locked may be too strong a term, for as soon as the pilot moves the thrust levers, the engine thrust will try match the actual thrust lever position. Therefore when a failure occurs, the ECAM step says "THRUST LOCK, THR LEVERS ... MOVE". Because there has been no actual change in engine thrust, this could otherwise easily go unnoticed. To remind the pilot that manual control must be taken, a single chime will sound every 5 seconds until the thrust levers are moved (at which point the thrust will match the new position) or the disconnect button is pressed, in which case the thrust will also match the thrust lever position—climb.

There is an automatic thrust function called Alpha Floor that is worth mentioning as well, though it was not a factor on AF447. It is a protection built into the autothrust system instead of the flight controls.

Alpha Floor will automatically select TOGA power when a set of continuously monitored parameters detects a pending high angle of attack situation, regardless of the actual position of the thrust levers. Its purpose is to initiate a preventive recovery before the situation becomes critical. The activation threshold is calculated such that aggressive maneuvering will trigger its activation at a higher speed than a slow speed decay. It is only operable in Normal Law, above 100 feet, below Mach .53, and only when the autothrust is operational. Once activated and the triggering parameters are no longer present, the thrust mode reverts to Thrust Lock, with the thrust set at TOGA regardless of the thrust lever position. Thrust lock is then disengaged by disconnecting the autothrust.

On AF447, seven seconds prior to the disconnection of the autopilot and autothrust, the crew had elected to slow down slightly due to turbulence. As a result, the engine power reduced from the normal 95% N_1[25] setting for cruise to 84% N_1 in order to accomplish the speed reduction. When the autothrust disconnected moments later, the power remained there while in thrust-lock mode.

15 seconds after the autothrust disconnected, the disconnect button was used to deactivate the thrust lock. This commanded the engines to climb power (where the thrust levers were positioned), which is not significantly more than normal cruise power at that altitude. 20 seconds later the thrust levers were reduced for about 7 seconds before they were advanced to TOGA.

---

25   Engine speed is measured in percent RPM of the fan stage of the engine, commonly referred to as N1.

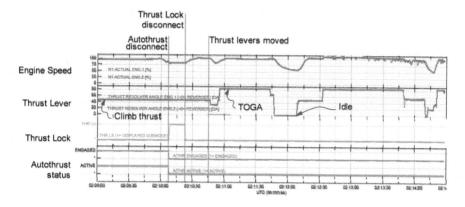

When the flap handle is out of the UP position (i.e., flaps out), positioning the thrust levers to TOGA commands full power and also commands the go-around mode in the autoflight system. The go-around commands a pitch up from the flight directors and autopilot (if on). If the flap handle is up, the flight director/autopilot mode does not change—only full power is commanded. At 35,000 feet, selecting TOGA provides only a small increase in power above the cruise setting, and no more than the climb setting. It does not result in a rapid acceleration or a noticeable pitch up.

About a minute after the autopilot disconnected, after a stall warning was received, the thrust levers were positioned to TOGA. Shortly thereafter with the stall warning sounding repeatedly, First Officer Bonin—the pilot flying, stated "I'm in TOGA, huh?"

In the Popular Mechanics article "What really happened aboard Air France 447" author Jeff Wise states:

> Bonin's statement here offers a crucial window onto his reasoning. TOGA is an acronym for Take Off, Go Around. When a plane is taking off or aborting a landing—going around—it must gain both speed and altitude as efficiently as possible. At this critical phase of flight, pilots are trained to increase engine speed to the TOGA level and raise the nose to a certain pitch angle.

I disagree with his assessment. 20 seconds earlier Bonin had also commented "we're in climb." I believe both statements refer only to the position of the thrust levers, not attempting to perform a go-around maneuver.

The stall warning announced "STALL" five times before Bonin positioned the thrust levers to TOGA, and continued to sound afterwards. It is apparent that he expected the application of TOGA thrust to accelerate the airplane out of the stall situation on its own, like it can at low altitude. He appeared to be completely puzzled why this did not solve the problem. He had forgotten that a stall is primarily an angle of attack problem, not a power problem.

Commentary on Design Flaws

Few machines from the simplest screwdriver to the most sophisticated jet airliner could not use a little tweaking here and there.

More than a few have claimed that the airplane suffered from "design flaws," but they were often unable to articulate exactly what those "flaws" were, though they generally revolved around the design philosophy of the fly-by-wire system.

It is my contention that simply designing a system differently than the commenter prefers is not by itself a design flaw.

Additionally, a system that shuts itself off when it is designed to shut itself off, due to a lack of data or failure of another part, does not necessarily constitute a "failure." We see this in the AF447 case when the flight directors are removed from view. The autopilot, flight directors, and autothrust did not "fail." They suffered from a loss of data required to operate. When that data became available again, the flight directors were displayed again, as per design.

Chapter 7: Stalling and Falling

After the autopilot disconnected at 02:10:05, the remainder of the flight can be divided into four phases characterized by pilot actions and trends of pitch attitude, vertical speed, altitude, and angle of attack. These phases are derived from my own analysis, as follows:

Phase 1: A period of 20 seconds from 02:10:07–02:10:27, starting two seconds after the autopilot disconnected where large lateral and almost exclusively, nose-up pitch inputs were made. Pitch attitude increased up to 12°, vertical speed rose up to 6,900 ft/min, altitude increased from 35,000 ft to 36,200 ft, and angle of attack, while higher than normal, was only momentarily high enough to meet the stall warning threshold—but not actually stalling.

Phase 2: A period of 23 seconds from 02:10:27–02:10:50. Roll oscillations continued, but the pitch inputs were mostly nose down, the pitch attitude decreased from 12° to 6°, vertical speed reduced to 1,100 ft/min, and altitude continued to rise through 37,500 ft. The bank angle came under control for the last 10 seconds, angle of attack remained below the stall warning threshold, and the stall warning remained off.

Phase 3: A period of 24 seconds from 02:10:50–02:11:14. In this phase the airplane was too slow for the power available. Altitude was fairly constant but at the cost of decaying airspeed, a rapidly increasing angle of attack, and critically decaying controllability. Pitch attitude increased and approached 18°, vertical speed ranged from near zero to 750 ft/min up then back to zero, and altitude peaked at 37,924. Roll began to destabilize again and large lateral inputs were made. The stall warning was on during this entire period.

Phase 4: The remaining 3 minutes 14 seconds of the flight starting at 02:11:14. The descent from the peak altitude began. Mostly nose-up inputs were made, often with full back stick, the pitch attitude oscillated, and the airplane became deeply stalled as angles of attack quickly reached and remained above 30°, reaching as high as 60°. All the while the airplane banked both left and to over 40° to the right. Controllability was extremely compromised as the PF struggled to keep the airplane right side up. He used full left and right stick inputs to counteract the extreme rolling motion of the airplane. Along with the rolling motion, the airplane yawed back and forth as it oscillated in pitch, roll, and yaw like a falling maple leaf. The yaw damper automatically counteracted each yaw motion with rudder commands within its limited authority. It was possibly the only thing keeping the airplane from entering a spin. Extreme vertical speeds of over 15,0000 ft/min were encountered as the airplane literally fell out of the sky. The stall warning sounded for the first 30 seconds of this phase and was intermittent thereafter.

Recovery Possibilities

Above all, this is a stall accident. Initial prevention of the stall was possible. This is proven by a number of other flights with the same malfunction that maintained control, often with little effort. All indications show that the pitch up that resulted in the loss of airspeed and excessive angles of attack were pilot induced. With each successive phase, prevention or recovery from the stall required more deliberate action.

In phase 1, simply correcting the pitch attitude back to level flight would have been enough to restore normal flight. Sufficient airspeed remained in order to maintain altitude. Recovery would have required releasing aft stick input and pushing forward to pitch the nose down to the normal cruise pitch attitude. Due to the fly-by-wire flight control laws, the airplane would not pitch down on its own if the sidestick was released. The pitch attitude and extreme climb would remain unless positive corrective action was taken.

The right and left rolling motion increased the difficulty of recovery. What may have been initially set off by the outside environment, was prolonged by excessive pilot inputs and the nearly double-the-normal roll rates available due to Alternate 2 control law. Roll attitudes never exceeded 11°, yet full or near-full sidestick deflection to each side was used several times to counter rolling motions.

The struggle to regain control over the roll may have contributed to the inattention given to pitch, which resulted in a vertical speed of 6,900 feet per minute at the end of phase 1.

In phase 2, sidestick inputs oscillated in both pitch and roll, with some correlation between pulling back with left stick input and pushing forward with right stick input. On average, more nose down inputs were made by the pilot flying and as a result, both the pitch attitude and vertical speed reduced. As the rolling motion came under control, pitch oscillations also stabilized at a pitch attitude of about 6° nose up. But that attitude was insufficient to complete the recovery and the airplane continued to climb and lose energy, though it remained below the stall angle of attack. Recovery would have required continued nose down inputs to lower the nose more and a return to the previous cruise altitude or below in order to regain airspeed needed to maintain level flight.

In phase 3 the airspeed had become dangerously low and the pitch attitude and angle of attack increased while the altitude changed little. The stall warning sounded continuously and the airplane reached the stall angle of attack. At this point a recovery would have required a more aggressive pitch down maneuver, first to recover from the stall and then a fairly steep descent of perhaps 5,000 feet to regain airspeed. The pull up to level off would then need to be gentle to prevent a secondary stall during the level-off maneuver.

Once the airplane entered phase 4 it is unknown if a recovery was possible. The BEA's final report on the accident says that by the time the captain returned to the cockpit (30 seconds into phase 4) that it was, "already too late, given the airplane's conditions at that time, to recover control of it." Airbus test pilots that I spoke to had only reached a 14° angle of attack at altitude, and would not speculate on the recovery possibilities beyond that. For most of phase 4, the angle of attack for

AF447 was between 30° and 60°.

The effectiveness of the flight controls was severely compromised by the poor airflow around them. The ailerons, at the trailing edge of the fully stalled surface, had no effect on correcting the bank, even at prolonged full deflection.

John Foster, an engineer at the Vehicle Dynamics Branch at NASA Langley Research Center, says that transport category airplanes with this configuration (non T-tail), typically exhibit good nose down pitch response from any AOA. Indeed, the pitch controls were quite effective in creating the very high angle of attack situation. The flight recordings indicate that there was some flight control responsiveness in pitch when forward stick input was applied, even at very high angles of attack. Unfortunately, those commands were not held long enough. More nose-down control inputs and steeper nose down attitudes would have been needed in order to have any chance of recovery.

An additional factor in a required pitch-down maneuver would be the ability to pitch down enough with the stabilizer trim in the full nose-up position, as it was for AF447 from about 15 seconds into phase 4. In one of my own attempts to duplicate the situation in an A330 flight simulator, after the stall was fully developed, sufficient nose down pitch down could not be maintained by forward sidestick displacement alone. The nose did pitch down initially, but as airspeed increased, the full nose-up trim setting overpowered the nose-down elevator and the nose pitched back up. Even reducing the thrust to idle and increasing the bank angle had minimal effect. I can tell you, it was not a good feeling to be pushing full forward on the sidestick and have the nose pitching up regardless. Only manually reducing the trim setting enabled me to reestablish enough pitch control to recover from the stalled condition. This recovery consumed over 10,000 feet of altitude.

I am the first to admit that this attempt was well beyond the simulator's defined operating envelope and validated flight data. However, I don't find it to be unreasonable. It highlights the extra efforts that may have been required to perform a recovery once into phase 4. I had the added benefits of being in a non-stressful situation, knowing that the trim was full nose up, and watching the flight control display page when I thought of manually moving the stab trim. Of course, the crew of AF447 enjoyed none of those benefits.

Stall Warning

One item often cited in the opinion columns is the inconsistent operation of the stall warning.

The stall warning is a synthetic voice that says, "STALL, STALL, STALL". It is in English even though the crew spoke French. The voice is accompanied by a cricket sound and a red master warning light in front of each pilot. Unlike the stick-shaker stall warning found in many other transport aircraft, the Airbus stall warning does not affect the sidestick's input or feel. It is notable that the warning is auditory only, except for the illumination of general purpose master warning light. Pilots subject to auditory exclusion due to a highly stressful situation, may tune it out.

It is true that the stall warning did not always operate when the airplane was above the stall warning angle of attack. However, other than to select full (TOGA) power when the stall warning sounded at the beginning of phase 4, I find no indication that the crew acknowledged or acted to the stall warning in any other way when it was working. Most notable was the lack of any nose-down input in response to it. In fact, First Officer Robert, the most experienced A330 pilot among the crew, is heard saying, "what's that?" one second after the stall warning sounded for the first time, and later after another stall warning. We cannot be sure that he was referring to the stall warning, but the two first officers never mentioned the stall in their efforts to understand what was happening to the airplane. After the captain returned to the cockpit the stall warning was silent most of the time, possibly hindering his analysis of the problem, even though the airplane remained well above the stall angle of attack.

The angle of attack sensor is a weather-vane like device on the side of the airplane. There are three of them. They measure the angle of the airflow relative to the airplane fuselage and therefore the wings. Each sensor feeds its angle of attack information to an associated air data computer which then makes the data available to the flight control and warning systems.

Why was the stall warning intermittent even when the angle of attack was critically high? The warning is inhibited whenever the indicated airspeed is less than 60 knots. The design logic is that the airflow must be sufficient to ensure a valid measurement by the angle of attack sensors, especially to prevent spurious warnings such as alarms due to gusty winds and unusual vane angles while on the ground. When the airspeeds values from all three air data computers are less than 60 knots the angle of attack readings are therefore considered invalid.

The airplane's actual airspeed was never below 60 knots. However, there were two reasons that the indicated airspeed was below 60 knots, thereby rendering the angle of attack values invalid and inhibiting the stall warning.

The first is the outright blockage of the pitot tubes by ice crystals. This inhibited the stall warning for only about 7 seconds. The pitot tubes were blocked for about 30 seconds for the left side and 40 seconds for the standby (the right side instruments are not recorded), but during most of that time the angle of attack was not high enough to trigger the warning anyway.

The second reason occurred in phase 4 where the angle of attack was so high that the pitot-static system could not effectively measure the forward airspeed.

In the center of the graphic below the brown and purple lines indicate the actual angle of attack, and the green line represents the stall warning angle of attack. The period of 02:10:10 to 02:10:20 corresponds to when the PF aggressively pitched up after the autopilot disconnected, causing the angle of attack to momentarily exceed the stall warning threshold. The blue area indicates the time period where the stall warning should normally have sounded, but was inhibited due to low indicated airspeed as a result of the clogged pitots.

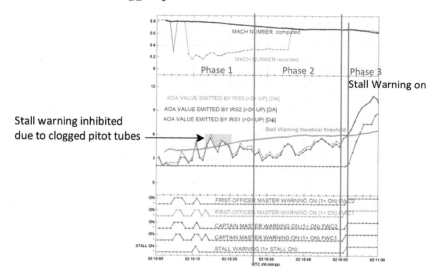

As the airplane climbed in phase 1 and 2, the actual airspeed and Mach number decreased. Along with a lowering of the Mach number came an increase angle of attack threshold for the stall and stall warning (the slower Mach number allowed for a higher angle of attack without stalling). Even though the angle of attack continued to increase throughout phase 2, the stall angle of attack also increased, preventing a stall from occurring. The airplane remained slightly below the stall warning angle of attack until phase 3, when the angle of attack rapidly increased.

113

At the beginning of phase three (02:10:52) the stall warning activated and sounded continuously for the next 53 seconds. The PF pulled back on the sidestick and pushed the thrust levers full forward to the TOGA position (02:10:56).

The stall buffet was felt, as recorded on the flight data recorder, and heard as a vibration noise in the cockpit. This buffet is a more rapid shaking of the airplane than turbulence. In the absence of the stall warning, the buffet itself should have acted as a stall indication to the crew.

As the aircraft's descent rate increased, the g load fell below 1g and a sense of falling would have been felt, like the initial feeling after pushing the down button on a fast elevator. As vertical speed continued to accelerate downward, the g load dropped further and larger nose-up inputs were made, probably to counteract the seat-of-the-pants feeling. Due to the combination of the flight control laws degrading to Alternate 2 and the loss of airspeed data, there were no protections or positive pitch stabilities to make the airplane pitch down on its own. Instead, the airplane attempted to follow the pilot's orders for an increase in g load, as commanded by the sidestick position, and pitched the nose up further.

The airplane's angle of attack continued to rise as the nose of the airplane porpoised between about 10° and 18° nose up.

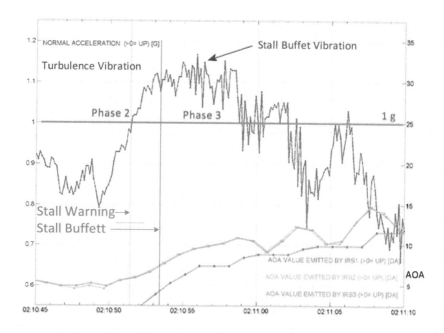

During phase three, the sidestick was held on average about half way back, telling the flight control computers to pitch up in order to provide a g load above 1.0. The airplane increased both the elevator and stabilizer deflection in order to comply with this demand.

At 02:11:10 the airplane's altitude peaked at 37,924 feet. The angle of attack was at 12° and increasing, and the g load was only at .75g's.

In phase 4 the angle of attack reached extreme levels and the stall warning became intermittent.

At 02:11:32 First Officer Bonin said, "I don't have control of the airplane any more now." His sidestick was full left, and remained so for 47 seconds. The airplane's bank angle increased to the right. This is possibly because the downwardly deflected aileron on the right wing caused its angle of attack to be greater than the left.

At 02:11:38, with the airplane descending through 36,000 feet, First Officer Robert moved his sidestick full left in an attempt to correct the bank angle which was approaching 30° to the right. He said, "controls to the left." It is not clear if Robert was commanding Bonin to let him fly the airplane or simply move the controls to the left to counteract the steep right bank. Regardless, Robert pushed his takeover push button, momentarily disabling Bonin's sidestick. But Bonin neither acknowledged the takeover nor released the controls. Instead he then pushed his own takeover pushbutton, disabling Robert's sidestick while he continued to hold full left sidestick. Then also moved his sidestick full back.

The elevator moved to full nose up to comply with Bonin's order. The stabilizer moved automatically to reduce the need for elevator deflection over time, and due to the constant up elevator demand, the stabilizer drove to the full nose-up position.

At 2:11:41 the stall warning was sounding when First Officer Robert again said, "what is that?"

Bonin replied "I have the impression we have the speed." Most interpret this to mean that he believed the airplane was going too fast, or that he had regained any lost airspeed—and therefore the stall warning was false. In fact, the exact opposite was true.

At 02:11:45 the angle of attack passed 45° and the stall warning silenced. The indicated airspeed dropped to 40 knots and the angle of attack information was therefore declared invalid. The low airspeed indication was not due to another pitot clogging problem, instead it was because the angle of attack was so excessive that it made the pitot-static system unable to measure the airspeed. At this extreme and oblique angle of attack, the air pressure sensed by the pitot tube was almost equal to air pressure impacting the static port at nearly the same angle. This canceled out the ability of the air data system to sense sufficient difference in pressure between the two ports that register airspeed.

At this same time (02:11:45) the captain entered the cockpit. He was not informed of the nearly 3,000 foot climb and he arrived to find the airplane descending through its original cruise altitude of 35,000 feet at 10,000 ft/min. The pitch attitude was 15° nose up, banked 32° to the right and increasing. The PF's sidestick had been full left and full back, and the stall warning had silenced.

The thrust levers were retarded to idle and as a result the nose pitched down from about 15° nose up to about 12° nose down. We can be sure that this was the result of the thrust reduction as the sidestick was held full back this entire time, and the elevators were at full nose up as well. The decreased pitch reduced the angle of attack slightly to around 38°, which was enough to push the indicated airspeed up to about 80 knots, revalidating the angle of attack information and activating the stall warning again. Meanwhile, the airplane was descending at 15,000 feet per minute.

Even though the stall warning sounded again, the sidestick remained full back, the elevators full up, and thrust at idle. The nose then pitched up to about level with the horizon and the angle of attack increased, causing the indicated airspeed to fall again and the stall warning to silence.

Almost 20 seconds later at 02:12:04 Bonin said, "I have the impression we have some crazy speed, what do you think?" and he started to deploy the speed brakes. This validates the theory that he thought they were going too fast. Robert commanded, "No, above all don't extend the …"

"No? Okay," Bonin replied.

"Don't extend," Robert said, and then they were retracted.

At 02:12:10, descending through 29,000 feet, the thrust levers, having been at idle for the last 20 seconds, were then advanced to the climb detent, and the engines spooled up. The aft deflection of the sidestick was relaxed, but the elevator remained full nose up. With the additional thrust from below the wings the nose pitched up from 10° nose down and reached 8° nose up over the next few seconds.

02:12:20 The bank angle, which had been to the right for the past minute, momentarily reached wings level, but continued to oscillate between 20° right and 18° left. Each rolling motion was counteracted with full lateral stick input.

02:12:33 The thrust levers were then pushed forward to the TOGA position again, but little additional thrust was available. The stick was moved halfway forward. The elevator moved from its full-up position, and the pitch reduced from 8° nose up to 2° nose down. The stab trim also started to move from its full nose-up position. The indicated airspeed rose above 60 knots yet remained below 80 knots, and the stall warning triggered again for about 2 seconds. This indicates that some pitch control, or at least pitch influence, was still available.

02:12:40 Another pitch oscillation brought the nose from 2° down to about 8° nose up and then about 8° nose down. The indicated airspeed rose briefly to over 150 knots and the stall warning sounded for about 5 seconds.

02:12:42 A brief exchange illustrated First Officer Bonin's uncertainty about the altitude. With the stall warning sounding, he said, "What are we here? On alti what do we have here?"

The captain said, "it's impossible," and Bonin repeated the question, "In alti what do we have?"

First Officer Robert replied, "What do you mean, on altitude?"

Bonin said, "Yeah, yeah, I'm going down, no?"

Robert replied, "You're going down, yes."

At 02:12:45 the airplane passed through 20,000 feet. The bank angle increased to 40° to the right and Bonin held full left stick again to try to correct the excessive bank angle. The sidestick averaged approximately neutral in pitch but the nose pitched down to about 8° below the horizon, as it rolled right. The airspeed rose, angle of attack data was declared valid again, and the stall warning sounded for about 10 seconds. With the nose pitched down and the stall warning on, the sidestick was moved further aft.

The captain and First Officer Robert instructed Bonin to 'get the wings horizontal' three times, and Bonin replied, "That's what I'm trying to do. I'm at the limit with the roll." He had been holding left stick for most of the previous 90 seconds.

02:13:00 The captain suggested, "The rudder bar. Wings horizontal, go gently, gently."

02:13:02 Bonin initially and briefly input left rudder to counteract the right bank, and as the wings returned towards horizontal, a right sidestick input was made and rudder input also changed to the right. The yaw damper's rudder commands intensified and Bonin's rudder input had little effect.

02:13:10 As a result of constant aft stick input, the elevator returned to full nose up. The airplane pitched up toward 15° and the angle of attack returned to greater than 45°, reaching even as high as 60°. [26]

02:13:18 Bonin remarked, "We're there, we're there, we're passing level one hundred" (10,000 feet). "What is, how come we're continuing to go down now?"

Robert instructed the captain to see if a reset of the flight control computers could help. The captain remarked that it "won't do anything," but he apparently reset PRIM 1 and SEC 1 anyway.

02:13:36 Bonin called out, "Nine thousand feet." The sidestick was still about half way back, the elevator and stab were at full nose up (trying to comply with Bonin's pitch-up order), and the thrust levers were in TOGA.

Robert said, "Climb climb climb climb!"

To which Bonin replied, "But I've been at max nose up for a while."

Realizing that Bonin had been doing the wrong thing for some time, the captain said, "No no no, don't climb!"

Robert said, "So, go down," and pushed his own stick forward for five seconds while the thrust levers were reduced to climb. Bonin continued to pull back.

---

26   As per phone conversation with Airbus experts on the accident.

02:13:40 A synthetic voice announced, "DUAL INPUT" five times, indicating that both sidesticks were displaced from neutral. Robert had failed to announce that he had taken control of the airplane, or to use the takeover pushbutton to cut out Bonin's sidestick commands. Bonin's nose-up and Robert's nose-down pitch commands canceled each other out. Robert commanded, "So give me the controls, the controls, the controls to me."

Bonin released the stick and said, "go ahead, you have the controls, we are still in TOGA, eh?"

At 02:13:49, with the sidestick held forward by Robert, the pitch attitude decreased to about 5° nose down. The indicated airspeed rose to about 90 knots and the stall warning sounded again. Robert eased up on the forward stick input and, despite having said he had the controls, Bonin pulled back on his sidestick for a few seconds.

02:14:00 The nose began to rise again

02:14:05 The captain said, "Watch out, you're pitching up there, you're pitching up."

02:14:07 Robert began pulling full back on his sidestick, saying, "I'm pitching up, I'm pitching up." The thrust levers were retarded to idle for two seconds and the nose pitched up reaching 16°.

Bonin added, "Well, we need to, we are at four thousand feet!"

02:14:10 The captain warned again, "You're pitching up."

02:14:16 At 2,500 feet above the water, and within the operating range of the radar altimeters, the ground proximity warning system (GPWS) activated, warning of the high vertical speed close to the surface. The synthetic voice said, "SINK RATE, PULL UP!, PULL UP!"

The captain gave permission, "Go on, pull."

"Let's go, pull up, pull up, pull up!" said Bonin.

The thrust levers were moved to TOGA both pilots pulled their sidesticks aft as the airplane pitched up toward 16°.

Bonin pushed the takeover pushbutton on his sidestick cutting out Robert's commands. "PRIORITY RIGHT" was announced by the synthetic voice. A red arrow in front of Robert illuminated and pointed to the right where Bonin was pulling full back on the stick.

Bonin, still not having understood what happened said, "[expletive] we're going to crash"

The GPWS commanded, "PULL UP!"

"This can't be true" Bonin said.

"PULL UP!" repeated the GPWS.

Bonin pled, "But what's happening?"

The captain commanded, "Ten degrees pitch." The GPWS continued to alert "PULL UP!"

Robert pushed his sidestick forward but Bonin still held the takeover pushbutton so Robert's inputs were blocked. Both engines were operating at near maximum thrust and the angle of attack was in excess of 45°. The airplane impacted the water 16° nose up, in a 5° left bank with a forward ground speed and vertical speed both at 107 knots (10,900 ft/min).

Were there more indications lost than just airspeed?

It is clear that for about 90 seconds, the crew of AF447 had a hard time determining if they were climbing or descending, as the airplane fell from 32,000 to 10,000 feet. Vertical speed indications were erratic. Most probably due to the effect of the high angle of attack on the static ports.

The following exchanges beg the question if the crew had lost more instrument indications than just airspeed.

PF: Pilot Flying
PNF: Pilot Not Flying
CA: Captain

	02:10:39	The air data and attitude/heading sources for the right side were switched to ADR 3 and IR 3 (FO on 3).
		"I don't have vertical speed indication. I have no more displays"
PF	02:11:58	At this time the airplane was descending through approximately 32,000 feet at 15,000 ft/min.
PNF	02:12:02	"We have no more valid displays."
PF	02:12:04	"I have the impression that we have some crazy speed, no what do you think?"
PNF	02:12:13	"We're pulling. What do you think about it, what do you think, what do we need to do?"
CA	02:12:15	"There I don't know, there it's going down."
	02:12:15– 19	The air data and attitude/heading sources for the captain were switched to ADR 3 and IR 3 (CA on 3).
CA	02:12:23	"The wings to flat horizon the standby horizon."
PNF	02:12:27	"You're climbing."
PNF	02:12:28	"You're going down, down, down."
CA	02:12:28	"Going down?"
PF	02:12:30	"Am I going down now?"
PNF	02:12:31	"Go down."
CA	02:12:32	"No, you climb there."
PF	02:12:32	"I'm climbing okay, so we're going down now."
CA	02:12:34	"You're climbing."
PF	02:12:42	"On alti what do we have here? In alti what do we have?"
CA	02:12 43	"It's impossible."
PNF	02:12:45	"What do you mean, on altitude?"

PF	02:12:47	"Yeah yeah yeah I'm going down, no?"
PNF	02:12:50	"You're going down, yes."
PF	03:13:18	"We're there, we're passing level one hundred."
	02:13:32	The air data source was selected back to NORM.

The crew, or at least the pilot flying, had an obvious difficult time determining if the airplane was "going up" or "going down." It is unlikely that he suddenly forgot how to read an altimeter. There is no mention in the report indicating the loss of indications other than airspeed. During this entire exchange, while there was confusion on whether they were going up or down, they were in fact going down in the range of 15,000 feet per minute. That is over 170 miles per hour— in the vertical axis!

I have spoken with some of the world's leading experts on this airplane, both test pilots and experts on its recording systems. They are not relying on the English translation of the transcript. There was no reason for the altitude display to have been lost. They stated that if it had been, there would have been other faults registered with the air data and display management computers, but there were none.

As they were descending through 30,000 feet, First Officer Bonin declared, "I have a problem, it's that I don't have vertical speed indication." In the prior seconds, the angle of attack exceeded 45°, and the recorded vertical speed had become erratic. In simulator recreations I have seen the vertical speed indication go blank when the vertical speed reached 20,000 feet per minute (shown below). I take him at his word that he did not have a vertical speed indication. However, all indications show that the altimeter continued to operate.

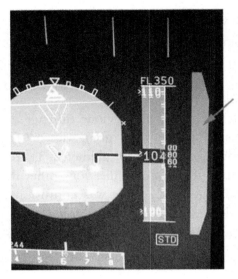

Blanked Vertical Speed Indication

The crew saw an airplane with operating engines, pitched up, erratic airspeed, an altimeter moving many times faster than they have ever seen one move, and a vertical speed indicator that was blank, erratic, or pegged beyond the limit of its normal display range. It most likely presented a picture that did not make any sense. The captain remarked, "It's impossible." This was a situation where they could not imagine that all of these indications were true, but what to believe? Alternate sources for the data were selected, but it made no difference.

There are also hints that the attitude displays on the two primary flight displays may also have been lost for an unknown period of time. However, Airbus and the accident investigators state that they do not believe that happened.

Both first officers declared that they had "no more valid displays." This is not a statement that would be expected with the loss of just airspeed and vertical speed. Then the source for the left side instruments, both air data and heading/attitude were switched to the ADR 3 backup, having been previously selected to the right side.

The captain said, "The wings to flat horizon, the standby horizon." Why he would refer to the standby horizon if the two primary attitude displays were operating is a mystery. The most logical explanation is that they were not working. No other similar incident had reported a loss of attitude display. That is until a Mihin Lanka A321 (Mihin Lanka is the budget airline of the Democratic Socialist Republic of Sri Lanka) in March, 2013. The airplane was en route from Jakarta, Indonesia to Colombo, Sri Lanka.

My sources revealed that the flight was cruising at FL 340, 500 miles southeast of Colombo, Sri Lanka (a position approximately 4° North latitude), and encountered turbulence at which time the autopilot disconnected with multiple ECAM alerts. The crew lost airspeed indications as the airspeed values fell below 30 knots. Altitude indications jumped 580 feet due to the loss of a reliable Mach value to correct the static pressures. The flight control law downgraded to Alternate Law and the autothrust was lost. The crew also reported the loss of both attitude displays on their Primary Flight Displays (PFDs) for up to 20 seconds. The loss of an attitude display in this type of scenario is certainly unexpected, and seems inconsistent with the condition.

A preliminary evaluation was said to have revealed that at least two of the three AOA probes, the total air temperature probe, and pitot tubes, and engine ram air pressure sensors had suffered an icing incident. But there was no evidence of any loss of attitude display as reported by the pilots since all the inertial reference data remained valid.

Perhaps the crew of AF447's apparent confusion was due to inoperative attitude displays on their PFDs, an erratic or inoperative vertical speed indication, and a rapidly declining altitude indication. We will never know for sure.

The BEA recommended that aircraft undertaking public transport flights with passengers be equipped with an image recorder that makes it possible to observe the entire instrument panel. This equipment would have clarified the "no more usable displays" statement and resolve questions such as the pilots reporting loss of attitude displays when the feeding data remained valid.

Could it Have Happened in a Boeing?

There were many voices that were quick to say that had this been a Boeing, with a conventional yoke control column and not the Airbus sidesticks, that the accident would not have happened. The theory being that the other pilot would see that the pilot flying was pulling back for long periods of time and corrected it.

We can never know for sure, but support of that theory comes from a segment of the cockpit voice recording when the airplane was passing through about 9,000 feet:

02:13:36 Bonin called out "Nine thousand feet". At this time the sidestick was about half way back, as it had been for the previous 40 seconds, though no one else could see this.

Robert remarked, "Climb climb climb climb!"

To which Bonin replied "But I've been at max nose up for a while."

The captain, realized that Bonin has been doing the exact wrong thing—despite prolonged stall warnings for some time, stated, "No no no, don't climb!"

Robert said, "So, go down," and pushed his own stick forward for 5 seconds while the thrust levers are reduced to climb. But Bonin continued to pull back. A synthetic voice announced, "DUAL INPUT" five times, indicating that both sidesticks were displaced from neutral. Robert failed to announce that he had control of the airplane, or to use the takeover pushbutton to cut out Bonin's sidestick commands. The result was that the two pitch commands canceled each other out. Robert commanded, "So give me the controls, the controls, the controls to me."

The excerpt from the flight data recorder tracing below, is from the time that the above exchange took place. The top set of lines graph the sidestick position of each pilot. Above the 0 line is nose down, below is nose-up command. The purple line defines the elevator position, which is at or near the full nose up limit at this point. The bottom line shows the pitch attitude. Keep in mind that about 3° is the normal cruise level attitude.

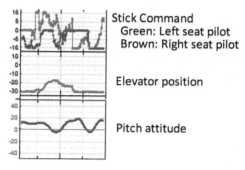

Pitch Control

When Robert took the controls, he did push forward on the sidestick, and the elevator moved out of full up where it had been for all of the previous 30 seconds, and most of the prior two minutes. The pitch attitude changed from about 10° nose up to slightly below nose level. However, this was not enough to recover from the stall. While the angle of attack remained incredibly high, it did reduce slightly. A few seconds later, Bonin pulled back on his sidestick again, counteracting the control inputs made by the Robert and the nose rose again, up to about 20°.

Would this have occurred in a Boeing with conventional yoke controls? It already has.

Northwest Airlines flight 6231 December 1, 1974. A Boeing 727.[27] This accident was due to pitot icing also, though in this case the crew had neglected to turn on the pitot heat. As the airplane climbed, increasingly higher airspeed was falsely indicated. The airplane stalled at about 24,000 feet and spun in at a vertical speed of 16,000 feet per minute. The instrument failure, pilot reactions, and resultant flight path are remarkably similar to AF447.

---

27   en.wikipedia.org/wiki/Northwest_Airlines_Flight_6231

Birgenair Flight 301, February 6, 1996.[28] A Boeing 757. In this case it is believed that the captain's pitot tube was clogged (possibly by wasp nesting) which caused the airspeed indicator to display increasingly higher airspeed as the aircraft climbed. Conflicting stall and overspeed warnings confused the captain who pitched the aircraft up, resulting in a stall and subsequent left engine flameout, whereby the airplane spun and crashed.

Aeroperú Flight 603, October 2, 1996.[29] A Boeing 757. This accident was due to plugged static ports that resulted in erroneous altitude and airspeed information. As a consequence of the pilots' inability to precisely monitor the aircraft's airspeed and vertical speed, they experienced multiple stalls, resulting in rapid loss of altitude with no corresponding change on the altimeter.

In all three cases the pilots focused on indicated airspeed and neglected the normal pitch and power relationship for their phase of flight. In the Birgenair case, the first officer's airspeed indicator was still working!

Those are just the flights that crashed. Other incidents that did not go so far as disaster have occurred due to airspeed errors with pilots not recognizing the mismatch between pitch, power, and performance.

If a red flag pops up on the airspeed indicator it is much easier to deal with than when the airspeed becomes erroneous over time. The pilot must have a base knowledge of what the normal parameters are, so that when things are not quite right, even with the autopilot on, the airspeed error can be recognized.

---

28   en.wikipedia.org/wiki/Birgenair_Flight_301
29   en.wikipedia.org/wiki/Aeroper%C3%BA_Flight_603

Chapter 8: Aftermath

At 02:14:28, quarter past midnight local time, the A330 crashed into the water at a 45° angle, 16° nose up in a 5° left bank with a forward ground speed and vertical speed both at 107 knots (123 mph, 10,900 ft/min). All 228 people were killed.

In the scale of things, 107 knots at landing may not seem high. It is less than the airplane's normal landing speed, and almost 20 knots less than the speed of the USAirways 1549 "miracle on the Hudson" flight at its touchdown.[30] However, it was the vertical speed on impact that destroyed the airplane. To put the numbers in perspective, the USAirways flight touched down with a vertical speed of 750 feet per minute. You would attain that vertical speed if you fell from a height of 29 inches; like stepping off of your bed.

Air France 447 hit the water with a vertical speed of 10,900 feet per minute. To attain this speed you would need to dive off a 500 foot (46 story) building, and that doesn't consider air resistance. Everyone on board was instantly killed with crushing injuries. The aluminum and composite airplane shattered on impact. Most of the airplane was on the bottom in small pieces, spread across an area a third of a mile long and 600 feet wide. Only the most rigid structures remained in large pieces. The complete debris field was considerably larger.

The Vertical Stabilizer

Among the first pieces of debris found floating was the vertical stabilizer. Many have contended for some time that the vertical stabilizer and rudder broke off in flight. The evidence cited was that these components were found floating, and apart from other floating

---

30   www.ntsb.gov/doclib/reports/2010/aar1003.pdf

debris. It was reminiscent of the American Airlines flight 587 accident in November of 2001, where an Airbus A-300's vertical stabilizer came off in flight.

Keep in mind that nothing of AF447 was found until June 6th, 2009, five days after the accident. Most of the airplane came to rest about 12,000 feet below the surface.

Certainly some items were broken off on impact, e.g., the vertical stabilizer and rudder. Others were likely shed as the severely broken up aircraft descended the 2¼ mile column of water, floating to the surface as the parts separated from one another and descended, all subject to the currents at each depth plus the time delay. It is no wonder that there was a wide dispersal pattern. If this debris dispersal pattern been on land, it would force a different conclusion, because the pieces would not have been moving for five days before they were discovered.

Furthermore, the currents in that area are not well known, and unfortunately search and rescue aircraft did not drop drift buoys upon arrival in the area. Drift buoys would have allowed searchers to track them by satellite to ascertain the currents, so that when pieces were found, the drift could be analyzed to determine a probable impact point.[31] Deployment of drift buoys by search and rescue aircraft is one of the recommendations of the investigation.

The vertical stabilizer itself shows evidence of damage in the vertical plane from forces that exceeded 36 g's. Symmetrical compression damage indicates that the destructive force was vertical, not lateral. Cracks and fractures in the structure itself, as well as the rudder/stabilizer attachment hinges bear this out. The center and aft attachment points took parts of the airplane structure with it. The forward attachment point was missing.

Consider that the airplane's vertical speed was over 10,900 feet per minute, or 123 mph in the vertical plane. Imagine what happens when a steel car is driven into a solid object (as the water would be in this case) in excess of 100 mph. It is no mystery that the aluminum and

31   AF447 Final Accident Report page 195

honeycomb tail should break off on impact with this tremendous force. The debris field on the ocean bottom reveals that the vertical stabilizer did not simply break off. The entire aircraft was severely broken up on impact, the vertical stabilizer being one of the largest pieces remaining. On the ocean bottom the main debris field covered a 600 x 1,800 foot area. Other parts scattered farther. A 20-foot section of the fuselage wall with 11 windows was found a mile and a quarter away. The few parts of the wings that were found indicate that the wings were completely torn apart on impact.

The vertical stabilizer is a mostly hollow, aluminum, honeycomb, and composite structure, with no heavy internal components other than three hydraulic actuators. It is no wonder that it would float.

This is in stark contrast to the American flight 587 accident, in which the vertical stabilizer separated from the aircraft in flight after departure from New York's JFK airport, and the airplane subsequently lost control. In this accident the tail was ripped from the airplane due to excessive side-to-side forces resulting from the first officer's "unnecessary and excessive" rudder inputs. [32] Tests reveal that the rudder input exceeded twice the design load limit. No fault was found with the structural integrity of the parts, though that did not stop people from blaming it on the composite structure.

The damage to the vertical stabilizer in that accident was quite different to that of AF447. Failure was due to excessive lateral loads, not vertical. The only thing in common between the two was that they were both Airbus vertical stabilizers that became separated from the rest of the fuselage, one in flight and one on impact.

The AF447 flight recorder tracings also provide evidence that the rudder and vertical stabilizer were intact until impact with the water. In the following parameter tracings you can see the direct correlation between the rudder commands, rudder position, and the resulting roll and drift angles of the airplane.

---

32   American Airlines Flight 587 Accident report, page 160

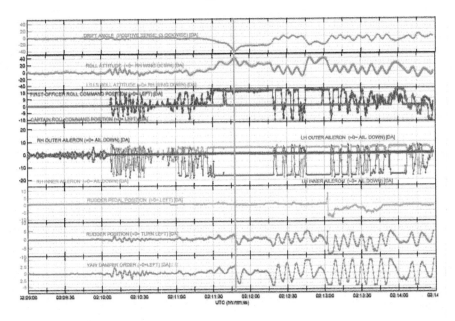

For a large portion of the flight segment the first officer's sidestick is moving left to right with corresponding changes in roll and drift angle. But during the periods of time where the sidestick command and aileron positions were constant, the roll and drift angles correlate to the rudder commands and position. This could not happen if the rudder was not there.

In the image above, I have drawn a vertical green line during a period of time when the sidestick input was constant, but the rudder commands and recorded position were in motion. You can see that there is a direct correlation between the rudder parameters and the resulting changes in the drift and roll angles.

Additionally, if the vertical stabilizer and rudder had separated from the fuselage in flight there would not be rudder position parameters to record.

I believe that it is possible that the yaw damper helped keep the airplane from spinning in, as two other pitot related accidents in Boeing aircraft had done (Northwest Airlines flight 6231, and Birgenair Flight 301).

Post-Crash Communications

Not having heard from Air France 447 from the time they were to have entered his airspace, the Dakar controller asked the Atlantico controller for further information on the flight, because he had no flight plan data. Atlantico supplied the data and the Dakar controller created a flight plan based on previously given estimates. But Dakar had neither radar nor ADS contact with the airplane and thus the flight remained virtual in his system.

At 02:47 (33 minutes after the crash) the Dakar controller coordinated with the next sector, Sal, with an estimate for POMAT (the boundary between Dakar and Sal control areas). Unknown to them, the flight had crashed 33 minutes prior. Dakar informed Sal that AF447 had not established contact with him.

Over an hour later, at 03:54, the Sal controller called Dakar to confirm the estimate for POMAT, which had been 10 minutes prior, and surmised that the estimate was for later. The Dakar controller said he would try to contact the flight.

At 04:07 the Sal controller was again in contact with Dakar again asking about AF447. He noted that he had established radar contact with AF459, who was 30 minutes in trail of AF447, but had not seen AF447.

At 04:11 Dakar asked AF459 to contact AF447. 11 minutes later AF459 passed the POMAT waypoint and reported that they had not been successful in contacting AF447, but had sent a message to Air France so that the airline could attempt contact.

Air France's Operations Control Center (OCC) attempted to send an ACARS message to the flight, but it was rejected.

There were a series of phone contacts between the Atlantico, Dakar, and Sal controllers attempting to confirm exactly where AF447 had been and at what time.

At 05:01 Dakar, still trying to figure out where the flight was, contacted the CANARIES controller in the area north of his, asking if he was in contact with AF447. He replied that he had no information.

Between 05:11 and 05:26 Air France continued to try to contact the flight over a dozen times via ACARS and SATCOM calls. Within that time the Air France maintenance deputy shift supervisor requested information on the automatic error messages that had been received from the flight. It was noted that the problem seem to be located in the pitot tubes, and there had been messages concerning the flight controls. The maintenance officer noted that he had seen similar messages before from airplanes passing through storms, but there were no communication errors reported.

At 05:23, over three hours after AF447 had crashed, Atlantico-Recife ARCC (Aeronautical Rescue Control Center) registered the disappearance of the AF 447 and triggered the Search and Rescue (SAR) process which consisted initially of gathering information.

At 05:30 the Air France OCC dispatcher called the CANARIAS controller, from whom he could not obtain any further information on AF447. The CANARIAS controller said that he could only contact the Sal center and had no contact with the Atlantico center. The controller added that given the time, he should have had AF447 in radar contact but that the flight was not in his air space or in Sal's. The CANARIAS controller and the dispatcher agreed to try and contact the Atlantico center and to keep each other informed.

At 05:37 the OCC maintenance shift supervisor and the maintenance center officer were anxious about the last ACARS message at 02:14 mentioning cabin vertical speed and the lack of radio contact with any control center.

At 06:35, after several exchanges between controllers, the Madrid controller confirmed to the Brest controller that flight AF447 was in the Casablanca FIR and would enter the Lisbon FIR within 15 minutes. This information was immediately transmitted to Cinq Mars la Pile ARCC and to Air France OCC.

Shortly thereafter The OCC told the Brest controller that the Casablanca center was in contact with the crew of flight AF 4595. This information was retransmitted to the Madrid and Lisbon controllers.

Three phases of alerts are supposed to happen when contact with an aircraft is lost:

- INCERFA (uncertainty phase), when no communication has been received from the crew within a period of 30 minutes after a communication should have been received.
- ALERFA (alert phase), when subsequent attempts to contact the crew or inquiries to other relevant sources have failed to reveal any information about the aircraft.
- DETRESFA (distress phase), when further inquiries have failed to provide any information, or when the fuel on board is considered to be exhausted.

But there had been some confusion about what agency was expected to trigger the appropriate alerts.

At 06:57, the OCC shift supervisor informed the CNOA (the French military body in charge of the aerial resources assigned to the French RCC) that Casablanca was not in contact with flight 447 after all. The CNOA asked if an uncertainty phase had been set off by a control center and if foreign search and rescue organizations had been alerted. The OCC answered that for the moment it was the control centers who were questioning the situation among themselves.

Between the hours of 05:30 and 08:00 numerous calls between the various air traffic control centers and Air France were made. There was no protocol between the various control centers to be able to make inquiries directly about the presence of an airplane. There were only protocols between adjacent control centers. At one point, the Atlantico-Recife ARCC asked the Air France station manager at Rio if he had the telephone numbers of the Casablanca and Lisbon control centers. He did not.

At 07:26, the Brest and Bordeaux center controllers (in France) were surprised that following so many exchanges between the various centers, no critical INCERFA / ALERFA / DETRESFA type phase had been triggered.

At 07:55, the Madrid duty officer and Madrid ARCC were surprised that everyone was requesting information on this flight but that no one had yet triggered the INCERFA or ALERFA phases. The air traffic controller questioned whether it was for him to trigger these phases. The Madrid ARCC pointed out to him that if radar and radio contact was lost a DETRESFA phase would have to be triggered directly.

At 08:00 (9am in Paris), Air France set up a crisis group.

At 11:04 the first Brazilian plane took off to begin search and rescue (SAR) operations.

From the last contact with AF447, it took three and a half hours before the SAR process was put into effect, and nine hours to launch the first search aircraft.

The failure of the ADS logon prevented the immediate alerting of ATC of the flight's diversion from the normal path and altitude, and delayed the awareness that the airplane was in any kind of trouble for almost three hours. The absence of position data that could have been transmitted by ADS-C contributed to the hours it took to fully realize the flight was missing, the five days it took to locate the floating debris, and the nearly two year delay in locating the sunken wreckage.

Due to the confusion and poor communications among the various agencies, the BEA recommended that ICAO ensure the implementation of SAR coordination plans or regional protocols covering all of the maritime or remote areas for which international coordination would be required in the application of SAR procedures, including in the South Atlantic area.

A more detailed chronology of the communications between the various agencies can be found in Appendix 4 of the final report, (SAR Communications) found at: http://www.bea.aero/docspa/2009/f-cp090601.en/pdf/annexe.04.en.pdf

ACARS Messages

When the aircraft was first lost, one of the only clues as to what happened was a series of maintenance messages automatically downlinked from the airplane in the final minutes of the flight to the Air France maintenance department.

Virtually all airliners use a system commonly referred to as ACARS. ACARS (Aircraft Communications Addressing and Reporting System) allows for message transfers between the airplane and airline, and some Air Traffic Control functions through the system as well (clearances, ATIS, etc.). The worldwide communications infrastructure is run by several companies that provide the ground radio stations, contract for communications satellites, and other communications services. On the A330, the aircraft's communications system can switch between air-to-ground VHF radio and SATCOM in order to be able to send and receive messages anywhere in the world. The system is used for a variety of purposes including sending text messages between the crew and company (e.g., dispatchers, arrival stations, etc), and automatically reporting takeoff and landing times, position reports, requesting weather, clearances, etc. Though voice radio relays and Satellite phone are normally available, most routine en route communications between the airplane and the airline are accomplished through ACARS.

In addition to the overt messaging between the crew and airline, a fair amount of other messaging takes place behind the scenes that is totally transparent to the crew. This may include such things as sending periodic engine data readings for maintenance monitoring of engine condition, reports of events such as pushback, takeoff, and touchdown times; and reporting of known maintenance events.

With the heavy amount of computer control and monitoring on the airplane, most maintenance items (failure, partial failure, abnormal conditions) are identified by the on-board maintenance computers that record and then automatically report these parameters and anomalies. In general these failures and/or abnormal conditions are then reported to the company maintenance department via the automatic ACARS messaging system, so that maintenance can better prepare for arrival and quick repair of the airplane and maintain high operational reliability. After all, it is much easier to keep the airplane on schedule for the next flight when maintenance can know about a failed component five hours ahead of time, instead of waiting for the airplane to pull into the gate.

Because the maintenance reporting system is automatic, it does not rely on the crew to transmit text reports of failures (though they may do that too). Additionally, the system can report on system issues that the crew may not know about because they are of such a minor level that the crew was not made aware of them. Some such items might be those that do not affect the operation of the flight and the crew can not do anything about anyway, but should be looked at by maintenance over the next few days.

Each item recorded is noted with the date and time, phase of flight (climb, cruise, etc), a system code number, and a general text description of the issue.

The maintenance reporting system is intended to keep maintenance personnel reasonably informed about malfunctions on the airplane. It is not designed to closely monitor the flight. Therefore, exact time recording (to the second) and immediate transmission of the messages in the exact order they occurred is not considered important. The messages may also be queued for delivery and transmitted when possible. For a satellite communication link, there is an exchange protocol that takes some time to establish and execute, and may depend on the availability of a signal and other higher priority data being transmitted or received. For example, an automatic position report was sent at 02:10:34 (30 seconds after autopilot disconnected) that took higher priority over maintenance message transmission. There was also a 30 second interruption of the satellite communication link about 45 seconds prior to impact.

When contact with AF447 was lost that night, the maintenance reporting system continued to operate until the time of impact. Before the aircraft and flight recorders were found years later, these messages were some of the only clues as to what happened on board the airplane. However, because the messages are only noted with to-the-minute accuracy, the exact sequence of two messages with the same time stamp cannot be assured. Nor can it be known, if all the messages that were going to be sent, were sent. Contrary to statements made in some narratives, these messages are not transmitted to ATC, or visible to the crew (unless they access the maintenance computer, which is almost never done.)

Except for the phase of flight digit, no other flight parameters are provided (such as altitude, speed, etc), so the picture it paints is one of individual data points often with insufficient data to draw definitive conclusions about what was really happening. The messages themselves also do not necessarily provide a complete picture of why it was triggered. For example, a system failure and a pilot turning off that system may generate the same message, or several similar faults may generate the same message. As if that were not enough to paint an incomplete picture, each message is only transmitted once, even if the fault occurs multiple times. The system also does not record or transmit when a system regains functionality, nor are all events recorded or transmitted, such as configuration issues, stall, and overspeed.

The messages are decoded below. Additional detail is provided in the first initial report of the accident. A brief description and explanation of the message's meaning follows each message below.

Example Message: (Spaces added for clarity) **WRN/WN 09 06 01 0210 22 10020 06 AUTO FLT AP OFF**

WRN: A warning, with some cockpit displayed effect

FLR: A fault not displayed in the cockpit (not in the example)

09 06 01 0210: Date and time stamp. In this example: 2009, June 01, at 02:10 UTC

22 100 20: A system and standardized reference number to a sub-system. In this case system 22 is autoflight and 100 20 refers to the autopilot

Added to this is a list of names of the other system identifiers that have generated correlated messages.

AUTO FLT AP OFF: The message text description including the system name: Autoflight, autopilot off.

An additional note of INTERMITTENT or HARD, indicates if a fault was transient or confirmed over a period of time.

Two times are provided below. The first is the time of occurrence transmitted with the message—with accuracy only to the whole minute, and the second is the time of reception—recorded with the seconds value.

Time of origination/reception: Message Content

02:10 / 02:10:10 WRN/WN0906010210 221002006 AUTO FLT AP OFF

Autopilot disconnection due to a fault (not pilot selected)

02:10 / 02:10:16 WRN/WN0906010210 226201006 AUTO FLT REAC W/S DET FAULT

Reactive windshear detection system is no longer available. Valid airspeed data is required for this system to operate, among other items, but windshear detection is only available at low altitude.

02:10 / 02:10:23 WRN/WN0906010210 279100506 F/CTL ALTN LAW

The change from Normal to Alternate Law 2

02:10 / 02:10:29 WRN/WN0906010210 228300206 FLAG ON CAPT PFD SPD LIMIT

02:10 / 02:10:41 WRN/WN0906010210 228301206 FLAG ON F/O PFD SPD LIMIT

The speed limits on the airspeed scales were no longer displayed, and were replaced by fault flags. The airspeed itself was most likely still displayed (though incorrect at this time)

02:10 / 02:10:47 WRN/WN0906010210 223002506 AUTO FLT A/THR OFF

Autothrust disconnection due to a fault (not pilot selected)

02:10 / 02:10:54 WRN/WN0906010210 344300506 NAV TCAS FAULT

The Traffic Collision Avoidance System (TCAS) is inoperative, possibly due to an internal reasonableness check of altitude change rate. A TCAS system considers the extreme altitude change in the short amount of time as a possible data error. Indeed, the vertical speed had been as high as 6,900 ft/min, at that point, an unreasonable vertical speed for cruise altitude. It could also be due to the lack of reliable air data. Due to the lack of a precise time stamp it may be impossible to tell.

02:10 / 02:11:00 WRN/WN0906010210 228300106 FLAG ON CAPT PFD FD

02:10 / 02:11:15 WRN/WN0906010210 228301106 FLAG ON F/O PFD FD

Both the captain's and first officer's flight directors while selected on, are no longer displayed, but replaced by a red FD on the primary flight display (PFD). The fact that they remained selected on set the stage for the flight directors to automatically reappear shortly thereafter in an undesirable mode.

02:10 / 02:11:21 WRN/WN0906010210 272302006 F/CTL RUD TRV LIM FAULT

The unavailability of the rudder-deflection-limit calculation function. The rudder travel limit value remained frozen at the current value at the time of the failure (until the slats extension command is given). Normally the maximum rudder deflection is reduced at higher speeds. The rudder and yaw damper remain functional, but the lack of reliable airspeed data makes the automatic adjustment of the amount of rudder displacement with rudder pedal movement impossible.

02:10 / 02:11:27 WRN/WN0906010210 279045506
MAINTENANCE STATUS EFCS 2

02:10 / 02:11:42 WRN/WN0906010210 279045006
MAINTENANCE STATUS EFCS 1

EFCS is the Electronic Flight Control system. This level message (maintenance status) is not visible to the crew. It is related to the message below received at 02:11:55.

02:10 / 02:11:49 FLR/FR0906010210 34111506 EFCS2 1,
EFCS1, AFS, PROBE-PITOT 1X2 / 2X3 /1X3 (9DA),HARD

This indicates the system detected a change in the median value of the three airspeed sources of more than 30 knots within one second (it actually dropped from 274 to 52 knots within 3 seconds). That started a process where the system monitors the difference for a verification period (about 10 seconds). Alternate Law was triggered, along with limiting the rudder travel limit (which was not annunciated to the crew). The flight control law would have returned to Normal Law if the median speed value was within 50 knots of the original speed prior to the loss, at the end of the verification period. If the speeds remain outside of those parameters, Alternate 2 is locked on for the remainder of the flight, and the rudder travel limit fault is displayed.

02:10 / 02:11:55 FLR/FR0906010210 27933406 EFCS1
X2,EFCS2X, FCPC2 (2CE2) /WRG:ADIRU1 BUS ADR1-2 TO
FCPC2,HARD

This message indicates that primary flight control computer 2 (FCPC2) no longer considered the information that was delivered to it by ADR 1 (via bus 2) as valid. This indicates that the fault was not detected by any other FCPC during the three seconds that followed.

02:11 / 02:12:10 WRN/WN0906010211 341200106 FLAG ON
CAPT PFD FPV

02:11 / 02:12:16 WRN/WN0906010211 341201106 FLAG ON F/O PFD FPV

This indicated that the Flight Path Vector (FPV) display (if selected) would not have been available. Other flight recorder parameters indicate that the FPV was not selected on. While several anomalies can cause this (including a vertical speed of 20,000 ft/min and true airspeed of 600 knots or more) the disabling of the FPV occurred because the calibrated airspeed fell below 60 knots, which we know did happen (and it also caused the loss of angle of attack data for the stall warning). There is also a discrepancy in the explanation of the first interim report which said that the FPV must be selected for this error to occur, but that was corrected in the final report. It does not need to be selected on to generate this error message

02:12 / 02:12:51 WRN/WN0906010212 341040006 NAV ADR DISAGREE

This message indicates that the electronic flight control system (EFCS) has rejected one air data reference (ADR), and then identified an inconsistency ('"disagree"') between the two remaining ADRs on one of the monitored parameters (i.e., airspeed). This condition leaves the system with no known trustworthy reference for the value of concern. This would have triggered a reconfiguration to Alternate 2 Law, had it not already occurred due to a drop of the two airspeed values from 274 to 52 knots within 3 seconds.

02:11 / 02:13:08 FLR/FR0906010211 34220006 ISIS 1,ISIS(22FN-10FC) SPEED OR MACH FUNCTION,HARD

This message is generated when the Mach or airspeed values on the Integrated Standby Instrument System (ISIS) are outside certain limits. In this case, it indicates that the comparison between the static and pitot pressures were out of bounds (i.e., static greater than pitot.) At 2:11:40 there was a large increase in the angle of attack, and very shortly thereafter the two PFD airspeed displays fell to low values and then display SPD flags. The ISIS value reached zero. This indicates that the angle of the wind into the pitot tube and at the static ports is at such an extreme angle that no useful difference in pressure between the two was measured. In validation of this theory, when the angle of attack was reduced slightly, the ISIS speed rose and other speed indications displayed (flag disappeared). On the A330-200 in cruise flight, as a result of the position of the static pressure sensors (below the midline on the fuselage) the measured static pressure overestimates the real static pressure, therefore with the pitot pressure abnormally low and the static pressure erroneously high, the situation is set up for this error message. The flight recorder shows numerous periods of time where the ISIS airspeed indicated zero.

02:11 / 02:13:14 FLR/FR0906010211 34123406 IR2 1,EFCS1X,IR1,IR3, ADIRU2 (1FP2),HARD

This message was generated by Inertial Reference unit #2 (IR2) and indicates that it considered all three Air Data Reference (ADR) units to be invalid in at least one parameter i.e., airspeed, altitude, or vertical speed. An identifier in the message (not shown) indicates that IR1 had originally reported the problem but the investigation showed that it had not completed the verification period required to generate its own fault. The other identifiers in the message (IR1, IR3) indicate that IR1 and IR3 had also rejected the ADR units output.

02:13 / 02:13:45 WRN/WN0906010213 279002506F/CTL PRIM 1 FAULT

02:13 / 02:13:51 WRN/WN0906010213 279004006F/CTL SEC 1 FAULT

These messages indicate a fault condition in the #1 primary and secondary flight control computers. The second interim report stated they may have been manually selected off or be the result of a failure, but in the absence of an associated fault message, it is not possible to command a shutdown, that is selecting the computer to OFF would not have caused the message.

However, at 2:13:28, as the airplane was descending though about 10,000 feet, First Officer Robert said to the captain, "Try to find what you can do with your controls up there, the primaries and so on." The captain responded "It won't do anything." Yet, at 2:13:35 (six seconds later) PRIM 1 fault and then SEC 1 fault are registered. The ACARS messages are received 10 seconds later, 6 seconds apart.

When pilots reset these computers, it is the normal practice to do them one at a time and wait a few seconds. These two switches are also right next to each other, which to me indicates the likelihood that they were selected off in sequence left to right.

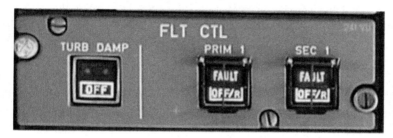

The third interim report also shows PRIM 1 and then SEC 1 fault status at this time. I believe that the captain selected these two switches off in sequence. It would not have solved the problem, nor have done any harm. This was never the problem, nor the solution. Additionally, pilots are not trained to reset flight control computer switches as a resolution to degraded flight control laws, especially when the computers have not indicated a fault by an ECAM message or FAULT lights on the pushbutton.

02:13 / 02:14:20 FLR/FR0906010213 22833406 AFS 1, FMGEC1 (1CA1), INTERMITTENT

This indicates a temporary fault within the Flight Management Guidance and Envelope Computer #1 (FMGEC) (the autopilot, flight guidance computer, and also computes some flight envelope parameters)

The fact that it was 'INTERMITTENT' means that the fault was detected for less than 2.5 seconds. The exact cause is not known, but it is theorized by the investigation to be the 'inconsistency between two channels.' However, the worst consequence of a failure, had it progressed beyond intermittent, would be the disconnection of systems (e.g., autopilot) that had already disconnected three minutes earlier.

02:14 / 02:14:14 WRN/WN0906010214 341036006 MAINTENANCE STATUS ADR 2

There are nine possible causes for this message but six are not relevant for this case, and three are linked to monitoring data from the three ADRs. The maintenance status portion of this message indicates that it reflects the initial stages of identifying a fault where ADR 2 is in a confirmation period concerning parameters from ADR 1 and 3. Therefore, ADR 2 had observed disagreements between the other two air data sources.

A fault message would have been expected but the airplane impacted the water before the confirmation period was over, and the fault message could be generated.

02:14 / 02:14:26 WRN/WN0906010214 213100206 ADVISORY CABIN VERTICAL SPEED

This message indicates a cabin altitude change rate of greater than 1,800 ft/min for at least five seconds. Right after the accident it was thought by some that this might have indicated an in-flight breakup of the airplane, with an excessive cabin altitude gained through a hole in the fuselage. While it is still possible that a hole could have existed to cause this, no plausible cause for such a hole has been theorized.

However, with the airplane descending at 10,000 ft/min or more it would eventually descend below the cabin altitude, which would have started out in the 5,600 foot range at cruise altitude and attempted to descend along with the airplane. But, because the normal cabin descent rate is only about 300 feet per minute, the airplane would eventually 'catch the cabin.' At that point the door seals, no longer pressurized from within the cabin, would release and allow air to enter the cabin from around each door. Also, the negative pressure relief value would open allowing additional air to enter the cabin to meet the 1,800 feet per minute down parameter. The timing of this message also weighs toward the 'catch the cabin' theory as the message was triggered after 2:14:00, at which time the airplane was descending through about 4,800 feet (below the original cabin altitude and at a high vertical speed).

Chapter 9: The Human Element

While the conditions of the intertropical convergence zone storm combined with the specific characteristics of the Thales pitot tube interior created the spark for the tragedy that ensued, the inability of the two pilots to control the airplane for one minute until the airspeed indications returned to normal is the agonizing tragedy of AF447.

The human element involves many aspects: pilot skills, experience, fatigue, and the ability of the brain to process information.

Return of the Captain

At 01:56 the captain rang the flight rest call button and a high-low chime sounded in the crew bunk. First Officer Robert's break was over and with the storm looming ahead, the captain elected to take his break on schedule. A knock acknowledging the call was made on the adjoining wall and heard in the cockpit. Three and a half minutes later David Robert entered the cockpit. Eight minutes prior to his return, the captain and First Officer Bonin had discussed how climbing was not an option due to the aircraft's weight and relatively warm air temperature.

Upon Robert's return Bonin had asked him if he slept. "So-so" was his reply.

"You didn't sleep?" the captain asked. Was he surprised at this?

Robert replied, "I was dozing, in fact. Are you OK?"

Bonin said, "OK."

It is not likely that someone would ask another person if they were OK, unless they had a reason to believe otherwise. This exchange may be a clue that either or both first officers were not well rested.

Captain Dubois powered his seat to the full aft and left position to allow himself to get out and Robert to get in. As the seat moved, its distinctive motor sound is heard on the voice recorder. When Robert took the seat, he never moved it any farther forward to the normal range. That would have been a comfortable position to sit in to put his feet up on the foot rests that hang below his instrument panel. His seat was found in the far back position in the wreckage. From this aft position it would have been very awkward to fly the airplane should he need to—and he would need to.

First Officer Bonin provided a minimal briefing to First Officer Robert prior to the captain's departure. The turbulence ahead and the inability to climb due to temperature were mentioned. Bonin asked the captain to remind them of the HF communications frequencies currently in use and assigned ahead. Captain Dubois provided them and then left for his break at about 02:02.

After leaving the cockpit, a pilot will typically use the lavatory, perhaps chat with the cabin crew for a few minutes before taking a nap in the rest area. As the captain is said to have had a companion on board, that would be another reason for him to not head straight to the bunk area.

Eight minutes later, at 02:10:04, the airspeeds become unreliable and the autopilot disconnected.

At 02:10:53, 49 seconds after the autopilot disconnected, the two first officers knew they needed help, and a call to the crew rest area was made, where they assumed the captain to be. Five more calls were made over the next 34 seconds. Unlike the banging on the wall that First Officer Robert acknowledged calls to the bunk with, the calls for the captain went unanswered. Robert asked "[expletive] where is he, eh?" "[expletive] Is he coming or not?"

The autopilot disconnect alarm is loud enough that you can hear it in the bunk, but not usually in the cabin. Had the captain been in the bunk and heard it, he would have known that was an unusual situation. Nobody turns the autopilot off at cruise, in fact in fact where 1,000 foot vertical separation of aircraft is used above FL290, its use is required.

Seconds after the autopilot alarm sounded, the airplane pitched up from 0 to 11° nose up, the g load increased to 1.6 g's, the vertical speed increased to 5,200 feet per minute, and the airplane roll oscillated left and right. The captain would have felt and noticed the increased g load of the pitch up and repeated side to side rolling motions. That may well have prompted his return to the cockpit without knowing he had bee called, to see what the heck was going on. If he was back in the cabin, and not in the bunk, he most likely did not hear the other two pilots calling the bunk area, which explains their frustration in the cockpit when he did not return immediately upon their calls.

At 02:10:56 a female voice was heard on the interphone saying, "Hello?, yes?" No response was given and the cabin handset was hung up. Three more calls were made and at 02:11:18 two knocks were heard on the wall. Two more call chimes were recorded and another female voice on the interphone.

At 2:11:42 the captain returned to the cockpit. He had been gone only 11 minutes, and only about a minute and a half from the first call to the crew bunk. I suspect he came back on his own initiative, for when he returned he did not inquire, "What do you want", but "What are you doing?"

In less than two minutes from the time the autopilot disconnected until the captain returned, the airplane had climbed from 35,000 feet to a few feet shy of 38,000, reaching a peak vertical speed of about 6,900 per minute (an extremely high and very unusual climb rate—over 10 times what would normally be used.) The pitch attitude had been as high as 18°, equal to the typical maximum pitch after takeoff.

At the captain's arrival, they were descending back through 35,000 feet and the pitch was about 15° nose up. The normal pitch attitude for this phase of flight is 2.5°–3°. The angle of attack had increased from about 3° to over 30°, but that was not displayed, and the airplane was descending at almost 10,000 feet per minute deeply stalled. In addition to the turbulence from the storm, the airplane was shaking due to the stall.

In response to Captain Dubois' "What are you doing?" inquiry, the two first officers stated, "I don't know what's happening," and "We're losing control of the airplane." Both statements were true.

Panic, Confusion, or Fatigue?

Several articles have concluded that 'Panic brought down Air France 447.'[33] While that makes for a great headline, I do not think it has been proven that an actual state of panic existed.

Panic is defined as, "a sudden overwhelming fear, with or without cause, that produces hysterical or irrational behavior, and that often spreads quickly through a group of persons or animals."

The final report states in paragraph 2.2.1, "In the first minute after the disconnection of the autopilot, the airplane exited the flight envelope. Neither of the two crew members had the clarity of thought necessary to take the corrective actions. However, every passing second required a more purposeful corrective piloting input." The report also referred to "the startle effect and the emotional shock at the autopilot disconnection."

Confusion and being overwhelmed by an unexpected flurry of alarms and alerts that simply exceeded the pilot flying's ability to cope with it all, is a likely scenario.

It was dark and they were experiencing moderate turbulence. No visible outside cues existed. Simultaneously, there was an autopilot disconnect siren, the "cavalry charge". The airspeed dropped low and momentarily disappeared, the flight directors disappeared. The indicated altitude dropped 300 feet due to the erroneous airspeed data. "Dings" sounded alerting the crew to the ECAM messages telling of the reversion to

---

33   www.ausbt.com.au/pilot-panic-brought-down-air-france-af447-investigators and www.huffingtonpost.com/jeff-wise/how-panic-doomed-an-airli_b_1135004. html

Alternate Law and the loss of autothrust. Soon after, the C-chord (indicating a departure from the selected altitude) sounded along with a synthetic voice announcing "STALL STALL." (which sounds like "STOLE" with a British accent).

First Officer Robert asked, "What is that?" What he is referring to is unclear, but he could be referring to the stall warning that had started sounding one second earlier. He had not had stall training since his A320 checkout nearly 10 years earlier. Additionally, "stall" is announced in English to the French speaking crew.

The flight controls degraded to Alternate 2 Law. In the roll axis, the airplane will no longer maintain a constant bank angle (or wings level) automatically. The ailerons were under direct pilot control. The roll sensitivity had nearly doubled that in Normal Law, up to 25°/second.

The airplane rocked to the right and required an immediate correction to the left. Why Bonin also pulled roughly half-way back on the sidestick is the great mystery. Did he overcompensate for the 300 foot loss of indicated altitude? Was he trying to recall the loss-of-airspeed training exercise performed months earlier? That event in the simulator was performed after takeoff, where the proper pitch attitude was 15° nose up. The proper action in this case would be to maintain his current pitch attitude of about 3°. It is likely the stall warning was never encountered in that training scenario.

He may have been trying so hard to control the roll, that the pitch simply went unnoticed until Robert pointed it out.

Having duplicated the situation in a simulator myself, the pitch-up action that Bonin used requires little effort and happens quickly. There are a number of alert sounds that go off and it would be easy to see how one would tune them out in an effort to load shed in what could be a quickly overwhelming situation. When the pitch up was first made, the stall warning sounded almost instantly, but only briefly. As the indicated airspeed fell below 60 knots, the stall warning was disabled. Once the g load from the initial pitch up subsided, it would have silenced on its own anyway, as the angle of attack returned to a normal range. Within a few seconds the pitch attitude was at 15° and the vertical speed in excess of 6,000 ft/min. Once established, the nose up attitude would have been maintained effortlessly (even hands off) due to the stability of the flight control pitch law.

Due to the loss of reliable air data, AF447 the flight control law degraded to Alternate 2 Law, and the airplane provided no pitch-down tendency on its own to help correct the errant control inputs and decaying speed. Airspeed depleted quickly as the airplane converted that airspeed to altitude, climbing from 35,000 to nearly 38,000 feet in less than 30 seconds.

For the crew of AF447, the ever-reliable flight directors disappeared and reappeared several times. But after the first time they reappeared, their pitch guidance mode had changed from altitude hold to maintain the vertical speed that existed each time they came back on. This was indicated, but it is easy to miss. The flight director commands are not recorded, but their commands were calculated as part of the investigation. Did Bonin follow them? The recorded pilot commands and calculated flight director positions seem to indicate that is a distinct possibility. The second time they reappeared the vertical speed was 6,000 feet per minute up, and that was the flight director target for 10 seconds before they disappeared again. Subsequent appearances provided guidance for a 1,400 ft/min climb.

Seconds later, Robert in the left seat was instructing Bonin, "watch your speed," who then replied "Okay, Okay, I'm going back down," but he did not.

Robert persisted, "According to that we're going up. According to all three you're going up, so go back down."

Experience tells me that when the flight director is on, it provides a powerful cue, and is easily looked upon as providing the right thing to do. But the flight directors, which do not give stall recovery guidance, continued to provide pitch up commands while the stall warning sounded continuously and the descent rate increased.

Their solution was to call for the captain.

The stall warning had gone off repeatedly and Bonin applied TOGA thrust. There was no increase in the actual amount of power. One minute after the autopilot disconnected, the stall warning sounded continuously. Bonin said, "I'm in TOGA, eh." It is apparent that he was expecting to power the airplane out of the stall situation like it can at 5,000 feet. Selecting TOGA at that high of an altitude provides only minimal additional power above the cruise setting, and no more than the climb setting that the thrust levers had been at. It is as though he had forgotten what a stall is and learned the wrong lesson on what causes the recovery to work. A stall is most effectively recovered with a pitch reduction to quickly reduce the angle of attack. Power, especially the minimal increase available at that altitude is not going to make any significant difference.

Attempting to level off as the altitude approached 38,000 feet only resulted in the continuing loss of airspeed. In that condition it is aerodynamically impossible to increase or even maintain airspeed with the available thrust. The decaying airspeed, and lack of nose down command sufficient to reduce the angle of attack, only resulted in a rapidly increasing angle of attack as the stall deepened. Soon after, the attempt to maintain altitude degraded into a rapidly increasing descent despite a somewhat constant nose up attitude. Reducing the thrust, caused the nose to pitch down. The situation was then far beyond any training ever practiced in the simulator, or even imagined.

First Officer Robert knew what Bonin was doing was wrong. He could see that Bonin was having a hard time determining this for himself. Why did he not take over at this point? He should not have allowed Bonin's incorrect inputs to continue when it was obvious to him that the inputs were critically wrong and he could have done a better job. It was not until they passed 10,000 feet that the dire nature of the situation became all too apparent.

In response to Robert's command to climb, Bonin admitted he had been pulling back for some time. Only then did it reach a point where

Robert felt he must take over as Bonin had been doing the exact wrong thing for a long time without realizing it.

It is apparent that they did not trust the instruments. Robert switched the data source for not only the air data, but for the attitude and heading as well. This was not an annunciated step on the ECAM. There was no mention of an attitude failure. He just said, "I'll put you in A-T-T," changing the attitude and heading data source to another inertial reference unit. At this point he had given up on the ECAM procedure and was trying to think of things that would work. He later asked the captain to try to reset flight control computers. That was never a solution for Alternate Law, and it was equally ineffective in this case.

When the captain returned they did not provide a chain of events, they only said that they didn't know what was happening and were losing control of the airplane. Robert stated they didn't understand anything and had tried everything.

As the stall deepened the airplane began a very rapid descent. A descent many times faster than they have likely ever seen before. They must have thought, "How can that possibly be?" and the altimeter (if it was working) must be wrong.

At 02:11:58 Bonin stated, "I have a problem, it's that I don't have vertical speed information." The vertical speed at the time was in excess of 15,000 feet per minute. The vertical speed indicator has a maximum display range of 6,000 feet per minute. If it was operating, the vertical speed pointer would have been pegged at the bottom of the display and changed from green to amber due to the excessive value. It may have also disappeared altogether, as will happen when the indication is in excess of 20,000 feet per minute. A value the designers apparently assumed was too high to be encountered.

Even with the captain present, the three pilots had a hard time determining if they were in fact descending. At 02:12:27 as they descended through 18,000 feet at 15,000 feet minute, the flight recorder tracings show the indicated/recorded vertical speed to be erratic. Robert made contradictory calls: "You're climbing" then "You're going down

down down." Bonin asked, "Am I going down now?" Then the captain said, "You're climbing." They were not.

It is possible the "climbing" and "going down" calls refer to pitch attitude and not altitude, or the erratic vertical speed, but it seems clear that the crew could not get a grasp on what the airplane was actually doing and why it would not respond to inputs.

Bonin asked, "What are we here? On alti, what do we have here?"

The captain declared, "it's impossible." What did he see that contradicted what he thinks the airplane was doing that it would be *impossible* to be true? Could it be that he could not reconcile the nose pointing up, with full power applied, and an altimeter that was showing an almost unimaginable descent rate? He was also not made aware of the 3,000 foot climb, the prolonged stall warnings, and the 3,000 foot fully-stalled descent that had occurred prior to his return.

For some time they were battling control of the roll, trying to get the wings level, often with little success, despite full control inputs.

There were also the apparent contradictory indications from the stall warning. Once the angle of attack reached 45° as they descended through 34,000 feet, each time the nose pitched down and the angle of attack reduced, even slightly, it allowed the pitot-static system to measure more airspeed, bringing the stall warning back on.

Could it possibly have seemed better to them when the nose was higher and the airspeed indication low or blanked out, because the stall warning was silent? Did they somehow believe that the stall warning was erroneous? Other pilots who encountered loss of airspeed indications, and had transient stall warnings, reported that they thought the warnings were false, because they had not strayed too radically from level flight. For them, the stall warning was incongruous with the stable pitch attitude and power settings they had flown. The stall warning margin is narrow at that speed and altitude and is not difficult to trigger due to turbulence or minor pitch inputs.

They may have been so overwhelmed by trying to keep the airplane upright, by the other alarms, by trying to communicate with each other, with calls from the cabin, and calls for the captain, that the stall warning was tuned out altogether.

In the AF447 transcript, no explicit mention of the stall warning was ever made by the crew. However, the selection of TOGA thrust followed the stall warning by five seconds and remained there while the stall warning continued for another 49 seconds. Two seconds after the stall warning stopped the thrust levers were retarded to idle. During that time Robert exclaimed, "But we've still got the engines, what's happening?" The thrust levers were returned to TOGA 46 seconds later after a subsequent series of intermittent stall warnings, and Bonin remarked "Okay, we're in TOGA."

To me it paints a picture of an initial loss of situational awareness that they were not able to recover from until a very low altitude. Their loss of awareness of how they drained the airplane of energy in a 3,000 foot climb, and the apparent contradiction of a 15,000 ft/min descent with the nose pointed up with full power, made the indications of that descent incomprehensible until it was too late to do anything about.

Their actions indicate that they thought that all that was required for stall recovery was the application of full power, and when that alone was not working, they did not know what else to do.

At the heart of the matter seems to be the crew's inability to comprehend the situation. Could fatigue have been a factor in the crew's inability to analyze and correct the situation?

Even though Bonin deferred to comments and suggestions Robert had made (the presence of ozone, St. Elmo's fire, the slight diversion for weather), Bonin was the pilot in command. Robert would have had to reach a given threshold of intolerance before simply offering tips and observations to the pilot flying would turn into taking command of the airplane. By the time the captain arrived back in the cockpit Robert seemed to be a confused as anyone when he said "But we've got the engines, what's happening? Do you understand what's happening or not?" Only when Bonin stated "I don't have control of the airplane anymore now, I don't have control of the airplane at all," did Robert respond with "Controls to the left." This could have meant that he was taking over, but at the time the airplane was rolling past 30° to the right. Bonin had already had is sidestick full left, and Robert made left roll inputs himself for a few seconds. Bonin did not relax his full back and left inputs at all, and the airplane's bank increased towards 40° to the right.

It is possible they were too tired to be performing well.

The captain had allegedly stated at 01:04, "I didn't sleep enough last night. One hour—it's not enough."

About an hour before the loss of airspeed event, the captain offered First Officer Bonin an opportunity to take a nap. One must assume that he had some reason to offer this, such as him looking or behaving tired. The captain said, "Try maybe to sleep twenty minutes when he comes back or before if you want." Bonin turned down the offer, "Oh … that's kind" he said, "For the moment I don't feel like it, but if I do feel like it, yeah."

One might tend to conclude that Bonin clearly said he was not tired. After all they had only pushed back three hours earlier. But the captain followed up with "It'll be a lot for you." Thus apparently knowing and trying to convince Bonin that he had already had a long day and he was probably not well rested.

When Robert returned from his break and described his ability to sleep on his break as "so-so," he asked Bonin if he was OK. He probably had a reason to ask.

It has been postulated that once the A/P disconnected the issue of fatigue would have been overridden by the adrenaline of the moment. Maybe it did to a degree, to make them awake, and to give more strength to pull back on the sidestick, perhaps without even knowing it. This is the source of strength that allows mothers to inexplicably lift cars off of their children. But I do not think it is the source for better mental performance.

It is during these high stress events that we read of soldiers, fire fighters, police, and other situations of high stress where they perform under this stress not by working out the proper solution with clear thought, but that their training 'kicked in.'

As mammals, our hard-wired reactions to stressful situations are to freeze, run away, or fight back. Thinking of a brilliant solution to the problem at hand is usually not in that mix. The pilot flying needed to know to push forward on the stick, not more strength to pull back.

The two first officers may have been affected by a degree of combat stress. Combat stress has been defined as "The perception of an imminent threat of serious personal injury or death, or the stress of being tasked with the responsibility to protect another party from imminent serious injury or death, under conditions where response time is minimal."[34] I think it is clear that much or all of those conditions applied in this case.

Tunnel vision, auditory exclusion, the loss of fine and complex motor control, irrational behavior, and the inability to think clearly have all been observed as byproducts of combat stress. Consider the multiple alarms sounding (autopilot disconnect cavalry charge, stall warning, chimes, and the constant sounding of the C-chord). It is possible or likely that these were tuned out (i.e., auditory exclusion)? Bonin's overcontrolling the roll and pitch inputs despite admonitions from Robert to the contrary, build a case for the loss of fine motor control.

In 1950, S.L.A. Marshall's *The Soldier's Load and the Mobility of a Nation* was one of the first studies to identify how combat performance deteriorates when soldiers are exposed to combat stress. Marshall concluded that we must reject the superstition that under danger men can be expected to have more than their normal powers, and that they will outdo their best efforts simply because their lives are in danger. In many ways the reality was found to be just the opposite, and individuals under stress are far

---

34   www.killology.com/art_psych_combat.htm

less capable of doing anything other than blindly running from or charging toward a threat. Humans have three primary survival systems: vision, cognitive processing, and motor skill performance. Under stress, all three break down.

When Bonin's training 'kicked in,' it seems likely that the only training he had to deal with the stall warning was the application of TOGA power. When that failed, they were out of ideas and there was no mental capacity to reason out a new one. The next level down of instinctual reactions from him may have been to simply pull back on the stick.

The combination of the startle effect with a diminished mental capacity due to fatigue and stress, during a time when there was a need to think quickly and accurately, and/or call upon past training that may not have been adequate for this situation, may have led to the failure to maintain level flight initially, and then to the apparent confusion which inhibited their ability to comprehend and recover the airplane.

Training

Many comments have been made on various forums concerning the training aspect.

One of the factors missing in training and pointed out in the final report's recommendations[35], related to the lack of "specific and regular exercises dedicated to manual aircraft handling of approach to stall and stall recovery at high altitude."

All three pilots had their A330 and A340 training in the context of an additional rating, taking into account their previous A320 experience, and based only on the differences between the types. As a result none had done any stall training in a A330 or A340 simulator, because the protections, indications, and warnings between these three aircraft are virtually identical.

Stall training, not only at Air France but industry-wide prior to the accident, concentrated on stall recognition and recovery at low altitude,

---

35   AF447 Final Accident Report page 204

where those incidents were considered most likely to occur. Even though there had been stall accidents originating at high altitude (as previously noted).

While the principles of stall recovery are similar in both altitude regimes, significant differences between low and high altitude do exist:

- Significantly less excess power is available at high altitude, requiring recovery primarily with pitch for angle of attack reduction.
- A lower stall angle of attack at the Mach numbers experienced with high altitude flight, and consequently a narrower stall margin than at low altitude.

Stall training, however, focuses on prevention and recovery *before* the actual stall is encountered, or "incipient" stall recovery.

In stall training exercises, students recover at the first indication of a stall, that is the stall warning or perceived buffet. The simulator training is not carried into the full stall scenario, nor is the simulator designed to do so.

Prior to the accident most stall recovery training also focused on minimal loss of altitude in the recovery. Rapid application of full power was the initial action, and at low altitude the application of full power often solved the angle of attack problem by itself. Very little pitch down was required to make the recovery and altitude loss was minimized. But again this was recovery from an incipient stall, not a full stall. Pilots were taught to take action as soon as the stall warning or other signs of stall presented themselves. Also keep in mind that stall training in the simulator begins with "OK, we are going to do some stall training now," and it is not presented in the environment encountered by this crew.

Pilots are also taught that in Alternate and Direct laws the flight envelope protections are lost (as stated on the ECAM when the control law degrades), and that one must be more careful in handling the airplane. However, in the case of AF447, the stall warning first sounded momentarily at 02:10:10, almost immediately after First Officer Bonin inexplicably more than tripled the pitch attitude to 11°. It was silent for

38 seconds then sounded at least four times before TOGA was selected at 02:10:55. While some nose-down inputs were made, the pitch attitude continued to increase and sufficient stick input to establish a nose-down recovery attitude was not made.

The ECAM presented: "Alternate Law, protections lost." First Officer Robert only got as far in the ECAM procedure to say "Alternate Law protections, lo ...". The transcript reads "Alternate Law protections (law/low/lo)," indicating that the transcriber did not understand what Robert was trying to say. This message is one that would need to be relayed clearly to the pilot flying, and there would need to be assurance that he understood it, as it affects the way he flies the airplane. At the same time that Robert was reading that step, Bonin was asking him about the previous one, "engine lever?" That is because Robert's reading of that step was also unclear. So, it is not clear that Bonin, the pilot flying ever really understood that the airplane was in Alternate Law and that the flight envelope protections were lost.

During certification flight tests, the real airplane was not fully stalled at high altitude, and therefore data on aircraft behavior and performance beyond that was non-existent. It is impossible to create a realistic simulator model from data that does not exist. I have performed a high altitude full stall scenario in A330 simulators by two different manufacturers and each one behaved somewhat differently. In those simulators it took about 10,000 feet to recover from the fully stalled situation at high altitude. I have no idea of the accuracy of this in relation to the actual airplane's ability to recover from an extreme fully stalled situation at high altitude.

In later tests by Airbus, angles of attack up to 14° were reached with significant buffeting, and that was proved to be recoverable. The point at which it might not be recoverable is an unknown. It would come as no surprise to many if the airplane was not recoverable at all from angles of attack in excess of 40°. But during the flight, even though extremely high angles of attack were reached (up to 60°) whenever the sidestick was positioned forward, the nose pitched down and the angle of attack reduced. How much altitude it would take to complete a recovery is anyone's guess, but it would be many thousands of feet.

There is no training in spin recovery of airliners either. A spin is a result of an asymmetrical stall. The entire focus of training is to prevent those scenarios. In my opinion, AF447 may very likely have ended up in a spin had it not been for an active automatic yaw damper working furiously throughout the remainder of the flight to counteract yawing motion. A spin would have resulted in an even greater descent rate and a much lower likelihood of recovery on instruments alone.

There is an old saying that says, "A good pilot uses his superior knowledge to avoid situations that require his superior skill." Acquiring that superior knowledge is the trick. Memorizing the facts and answering the test questions does not always develop insight. In fact, it rarely does.

A pilot needs to understand the airplane, in all its modes. But that level of knowledge, understanding, and insight can be difficult to acquire in a short amount of time. There is a huge volume of material to be assimilated.

Like a surgeon that learns a new procedure, one does not become an instant expert. Once simulator training is complete and the new pilot is certified to fly the airplane, his or her initial experience in the airplane (15–25 hours typically) is with a line instructor, on actual passenger carrying flights. Most of that time is spent in cruise, and on a long-range airplane such as the A330, there will most likely only be a few takeoffs and landings with the instructor present before he is satisfied that the new pilot is "good to go." But the learning process is far from over.

The new pilot will be restricted slightly in the weather that an approach may be made in, and he will not be authorized to fly with another pilot who also has fewer than 75 hours in the airplane. It will be up to the pilot's own initiative as to how well he reviews his previous materials, and refreshes his memory of all the material that he had to try and absorb quickly just a few weeks prior.

It can seem overwhelming at first, so much to remember, so much to look for, so much to keep in mind. Until it clicks, and then the airplane is a beautiful friend to fly. But it will take a conscious effort to do it. If one only thinks about the routine functions used on every flight, some of the lesser used functions and nuances can be forgotten.

Everything works so well, so much of the time, that when things are not going right, it is easy to fall into the trap of assuming that the automation is doing the right thing. For example, that anytime the flight directors are on, that they are worth following.

There are red disconnect buttons on the sidestick (for the autopilot) and on the thrust levers (for the autothrust) that give the pilot instant control over the airplane. I have told my students many times, "If it's not doing what you want it to do, make it do it! Click it off, push it over, make it turn, whatever it is you want to happen, *Make it Happen!*" Of course, you must be thinking far enough ahead of the airplane to know what that is.

The Airline Transport Pilot (ATP) standards for the US dictate that the successful candidate must be the "master of the airplane." It is not just a skill set, it is also a mind set.

The Final accident report by the BEA states the following as a component of the cause of the accident:

> The occurrence of the failure in the context of flight in cruise completely surprised the pilots of flight AF447. The apparent difficulties with airplane handling at high altitude in turbulence led to excessive handling inputs in roll and a sharp nose-up input by the PF. The destabilization that resulted from the climbing flight path and the evolution in the pitch attitude and vertical speed was added to the erroneous airspeed indications and ECAM messages, which did not help with the diagnosis.

> The crew, progressively becoming de-structured, likely never understood that it was faced with a "simple" loss of three sources of airspeed information. In the minute that followed the autopilot disconnection, the failure of the attempts to understand the

situation and the de-structuring of crew cooperation fed on each other until the total loss of cognitive control of the situation.

The airplane went into a sustained stall, signaled by the stall warning and strong buffet. Despite these persistent symptoms, the crew never understood that they were stalling and consequently never applied a recovery maneuver. The combination of the ergonomics of the warning design, the conditions in which airline pilots are trained and exposed to stalls during their professional training and the process of recurrent training does not generate the expected behavior in any acceptable reliable way.

In its current form, recognizing the stall warning, even associated with buffet, supposes that the crew accords a minimum level of "legitimacy" to it. This then supposes sufficient previous experience of stalls, a minimum of cognitive availability and understanding of the situation, knowledge of the airplane (and its protection modes) and its flight physics. An examination of the current training for airline pilots does not, in general, provide convincing indications of the building and maintenance of the associated skills.

In the absence of reliable speed indication, an understanding of the physics of high altitude flying, gained through training in the fundamental principles of energy conversion, equilibriums of forces, and lift and propulsion ceilings, could have considerably helped the pilots to anticipate the rapid deterioration in their situation and to take the appropriate corrective measure in time: initiate a descent.

The final report theorizes that overspeed was a strong risk in the PF's mind. I do not disagree, as several statements were made about having a "crazy speed," and at one point he extended the speed brakes. This was the consequence of the fact that, in theoretical teaching (notably Airline Transport Certificate), the risk of "high speed stall" is presented equally with the more classic "low speed stall". Though low-speed buffet is quite well known to pilots, excursions beyond maximum speed limits are not demonstrated in training. Furthermore, vibrations (linked to buffet) were erroneously associated with overspeed.

Air France's Aeronautical Manual describes in great detail, over 38 pages, the physics of high-altitude flight with real cases. This knowledge is also included in the theoretical teaching that is supposed to be provided at an advanced stage in the training of a future airline pilot (Airline Transport License theory, type rating performance). The climbing flight path that was initially more or less deliberate on the part of the crew is likely a clue to the insufficient assimilation of these theoretical notions.

Modern aircraft such as the A330 are far less critical in the transonic range than their earlier generation counterparts. In those airplanes, an overspeed condition could lead to an aft shift of the center of lift, interruption of the airflow over the tail, and an uncontrollable dive, known as Mach tuck.

Unfortunately, the characteristics of exceeding the maximum speeds for particular aircraft types, and therefore the applicable risk for each, are not well known to pilots.

The Future of Training

Training has certainly improved with time, and I am confident it will continue to do so. There are areas that are subject to improvement, and I have no doubt that progress will be made along these lines.

A current threat is that a large amount of time is dedicated to simply learning to operate the particular aircraft and its technology, along with the company's procedures for the normal and non-normal operations as required. Little time is dedicated to flying skills, which obviously must be the foundation upon which all the procedural and technology training is based.

Pilots come from a wide variety of backgrounds. It is difficult to quantify what actual experience and skill any one pilot has in handling unexpected circumstances where control of the airplane is at stake.

Even if a pilot had the experience and skill when he was hired, how well are those skills preserved when flying on the autopilot 99% of the time for decades?

Loss of Control In-flight (LOC-I) remains the leading cause of accidents over the last 20 years. Other accident causal factors have been reduced due to more reliable equipment and systems providing improved protection and recovery from windshear, traffic, and terrain threats. Yet the LOC-I accident rate remains virtually unimproved and has been assuming an increasing percentage of the cause of fatalities. According to a Boeing study, there were 1493 fatalities due to LOC-I, one due to engine failure, and 225 due to non-powerplant systems failures (less than ⅙ of the LOC-I rate).[36] Yet considerably more time is spent on those failure scenarios than recovery and prevention of loss-of-control events.

In June 2009, coincidentally right after the AF447 accident, the International Committee for Aviation Training in Extended Envelopes' (ICATEE) group was formed under the Royal Aeronautical Society. The group consisted of more than 80 specialists from around the world. Their goal was to develop improvements in airline pilot training to prevent loss of control accidents in the future.

LOC-I accidents had been highlighted due to several recent high profile crashes: a Colgan Air Bombardier Q400 in Buffalo, NY, and a Turkish 737 crash in Amsterdam, Netherlands. They both occurred in February 2009, and both had been the result of improper pilot action that lead to stalls, though under different circumstances. Though they did not know it at the time the group convened, AF447 is obviously in that same category.

Results from more than three years of work by the group are due to be available in mid 2013, and are said to include a training matrix and an upset prevention and recovery manual. The group identified a list of shortcomings in training, including the limited environment pilots are

---

36 Statistical Summary of Commercial Jet Airplane Accidents-Worldwide Operations, 2002-20011, Boeing Commercial Airplane Group, www.boeing.com/news/techissues/pdf/statsum.pdf

exposed to in training, simulator realism at the edges of the envelope, g-force awareness, and the ability to create a "startle and surprise" environment in the simulator.

Sunjoo Advani, an aerospace engineer that headed the ICATEE, said, "As it turns out, one of the biggest problems is startle and surprise during unexpected and unforeseen events. LOC exposes [the pilots] in such a way that they have to go from a low state of arousal to a quick and effective response; and those responses can be counterintuitive." Included in those responses may be such actions as pulling on the yoke (or sidestick) after being startled, even though stall warnings are taking place.

In the case of AF447, we see the crew going from a "low state of arousal" (cruise flight) to the sudden and simultaneous loss of reliable indications, flight director guidance, and autopilot control, combined with no outside visual reference. Bonin's actions are often described as "inexplicable." In light of the work of the group, they seem almost predictable.

Advani said that simulator training can be improved by teaching pilots to recognize and recover at various stages of the development of an upset. "For high-altitude stall training you should not be putting the pilot in the simulator and saying 'recover.' Pilots need to recognize the signs, the buffet, the stall warning, the stick pusher, and learn not to fight those systems. These are basics that we have not adequately or consistently trained for."[37]

The training technique improvements are thought to be able to achieve about 75% of the goal in training improvements. The other 25% could be accomplished with improvements in the training devices themselves. The envelope of the simulator should be extended beyond approaching the stall, as the airplane's actual stall characteristics are not accurately represented in the simulators. The actual airplane's behavior tends to have a more violent buffet, and be less stable in terms of roll and yaw. One suggested method is the incorporation into simulators

37   Aviation Week and Space Technology, Amping the Envelope December 2, 2012

of a 'representative model' of a transport category aircraft's stall behavior. While it may not match the individual airplane model's stall characteristics exactly, it will be far better than the non-data the current simulator behaviors are based on today.

Additional simulator improvements could be functions that provide a clogged pitot scenario, wake turbulence encounter (which can often induce a rapid rolling motion), and other realistic models, in addition to the current menu of windshear scenarios that modern airline flight simulators offer.

But there are limits to what can be done, even in the most advanced simulator, as it remains bolted to the floor. G-load sensation is difficult or impossible to represent. Some degree of positive g's and accelerations are achieved by pitching the simulator back, but negative g's (lightness in the seat), and high accelerations are not possible to create.

To answer these demands, a real airplane can be used, and *is* being used. Aviation Performance Solutions (APS), in Mesa AZ, uses a fleet of aerobatic aircraft to teach upset recovery training. Their clients are largely corporate and private customers, but there has also been some airline interest as well. One curriculum offered by APS involves a multi-day, multi-flight regime. You can practice these maneuvers all day long in a simulator, but it takes on a whole new level when the airplane is pulling down on your seatbelt and objects are floating or flying around the cockpit.

In the aircraft, the trainees feel the real-life forces and cues, experience actual upset attitudes and need to recover. Then they are placed in the simulator again and can compare the best the simulator has to offer with real forces, and make the correlations.

Randall Brooks, in his paper *Loss of Control in Flight, Training Foundations and Solutions*[38] states:

> Although there is no technical challenge in creating a visual scene of a 110° bank attitude with the nose 30° below the horizon, the learning experienced while viewing that scene from the security of a simulator bay has no relation to the knowledge and attitudinal changes received from viewing that very same attitude strapped into an aircraft.

> The development and acquisition of skills related to correctly and appropriately responding to the psycho/physiological reactions inherent in confronting undesirable aircraft states is fundamental to executing a safe recovery from an unexpected aircraft upset. The required learning cannot be achieved absent from the consequences faced in actual flight.

> What this means is that some training in an aircraft is required to fully prepare a pilot for an aircraft upset encounter.

The addition of airplane training adds some additional risk. But the psychological impact of being in a real airplane in an actual unusual attitude that must be recovered from enhances the training experience, and hopefully its effectiveness. The additional risk is mitigated by specially trained instructors, in a structured training program, in an aircraft suitable for this maneuvering. While the addition of aircraft training will increase the risk for that training, it should increase the safety of airline operations staffed with those trained pilots.

In the decade of 2000–2011, almost 1500 people died in loss of control in-flight accidents.[39] If the fatality rate could be reduced by any meaningful measure by applying the risk to the pilots in training instead of the traveling public, it seems to be a reasonable thing to do. There

---

38   Loss of Control in Flight, Training Foundations and Solutions, Randall Brooks, European Airline Training Symposium, November 2010

39   Statistical Summary of Commercial Jet Airplane Accidents-Worldwide Operations, 2002-2011, p.22, Boeing Commercial Airplane Group www.boeing.com/news/techissues/pdf/statsum.pdf

are, of course, the cost and logistical factors of adding a completely new type of training, that is not widely available, and applying it to tens of thousands of airline pilots. It will not come without resistance from those paying for it.

ICATEE believes the current airline pilot population should receive dedicated simulator sessions in upset recovery training, "including specific elements that can create surprise in the simulator." It should be followed by recurrent training every 3–5 years. [40]

Creating an element of surprise in simulator training will not be easy. Nobody expects to go to a training or checking session and sit at cruise for 8 hours. The subjects to be covered are known to the trainees, even if they were not well briefed immediately prior to the training session. A degree of randomness in checking scenarios is often currently used, but the simulator's programming and the instructor's 'bag of tricks' contains only so many possibilities.

In 1985 we did not know how to train crew-resource management (CRM), threat-and-error management (TEM), or how to incorporate other human factors elements. All of which are integrated into flight crew training now. Perhaps techniques will be developed to better prepare pilots to deal with startle, surprise, working under high stress situations.

Enhancements to the simulators themselves to add additional faults (e.g., clogged pitot scenarios) and simulations of post-stall behavior will neither be easy nor inexpensive. Detailed analysis of incidents and accidents like AF447 by simulator manufacturers and regulatory authorities will go a long way toward making the simulators of the future better than today's.

---

40   Aviation Week and Space Technology, 'Amping the Envelope' December 2, 2012

Chapter 10: Lessons Learned

There is much to be learned from almost every accident and the loss of AF447 is no exception. This accident centered around a loss of control at altitude. According to the British Civil Aviation Authority, loss of control events have been identified globally as the current most serious risk to flight safety—and the biggest single cause of commercial air accidents over recent years. Loss of control often follows a partial or full stall to an aircraft.

Many of the largest threats of the past such as controlled flight into terrain, windshear, and mechanical failure have been very successfully reduced with improved Ground Proximity Warning Systems (GPWS), improved airborne weather radar, windshear detection and recovery guidance, and improved engineering.

High Altitude Stalls

Clearly this is a stall accident. All of the major aircraft manufacturers have updated their stall recovery procedures to emphasize reducing angle of attack as the immediate and primary means of stall recovery, with power application only after control is assured. These revised procedures also acknowledge that high power settings on airplanes with low hung engines may in some instances be contrary to the ability to reduce angle of attack effectively. We have seen, in this case, how at one point the reduction of power caused the nose to pitch down and angle of attack to reduce. Unfortunately, the pilots were acting contrary to the required inputs to complete the recovery.

Primary flight students are taught that an airplane always stalls at the same angle of attack. That is true enough within the operational envelope of a single-engine Cessna. However, when the effects of high speed flight are concerned, where speed is measured in Mach number, we find that airplanes *do not* always stall at the same angle of attack. The stall angle of attack at high speeds due to the compressibility of the air at high speeds (and some egghead fluid-dynamics factors) is significantly lower, on the order of 5°–6° at Mach .80, where the cruise AOA is about 2.5°. This means the maneuver margin is significantly reduced. You cannot yank on the stick like you can at 5,000 feet.

This narrowed stall margin is reflected in what jet pilots refer to as the "buffet margin." At low altitudes we have a 2.5 g limit and can maneuver freely within that range with no stall warning. The 2.5 value is also a structural load limit, in many scenarios the stall limit would be higher. At altitude we see only 1.3 or 1.5 g margin is available before stall. (Thus, a .3 g margin from normal 1 g flight, vs. 1.5+ g margin at low altitudes and speeds—a factor of five!) Pilots must be gentler on pitch maneuvers at high altitudes to avoid stall.

For Airbus pilots, Normal Law normally provides protection, but not Alternate Law. As a result, Airbus has increased the stall warning margin a bit in this regime to provide adequate warning. As explained earlier, there is a very narrow angle of attack margin between cruise and stall warning. One result of this is that when flying in Alternate Law in turbulence, the stall warning may sound momentarily with vertical gusts. It should warn the pilot to continue to maneuver with care, as a stall is not far away, even though recovery action is not necessary for these transient warnings.

Pair this concept with the fact that there is significantly less "excess" power available at altitude. In cruise there is little difference between cruise power and full power. Contrast this with the low altitude regime where application of TOGA thrust imparts a significant power addition and allows the possibility of "powering out" of a stall situation. No such ability exists in the high altitude/high Mach arena. At a given point on the drag curve, it is impossible to accelerate in level flight with the available power alone. Therefore, stall recovery *must* be accomplished with a reduction in pitch to lower the angle of attack. If airspeed has been lost, there is little excess power to regain it with, the only available source of energy, even once the AOA has been reduced, is to trade altitude for airspeed.

There is a reason that pilots are taught stall recognition and recovery from *incipient* stalls. We do not take airliners into a full stall, even in a simulator. The point is to recognize the warning signs (stall warning, buffet, sloppy control response) and recover *before* a full stall is reached. In the AF447 case, all the warning signs were ignored. Once the angle of attack was exceptionally high, it would have taken a large prolonged nose down movement to correct that, perhaps exceeded 35° below the horizon to get the AOA back in the normal range. This crew fought nose down attitudes of 8° below the horizon with full back stick.

Once the AOA is corrected, if a significant nose down attitude is required, the pilot must be careful in bringing the nose back up to level flight. The stall margin is small, and as the speed increases, the stall margin narrows further; therefore, the pull up must be made gently enough to avoid a secondary stall.

Understanding the Flight Control Laws

Pilots must understand their airplane. Not just enough to pass the test, but every day.

For the Airbus pilot, he must understand what the sidestick is commanding in whatever flight-control law the airplane is operating in. My experience is that, when asked, most Airbus pilots need to think about this one for a few seconds before answering.

In Alternate 1 the roll control is also the same as Normal Law (roll rate demand). When the sidestick is centered, the flight control system will attempt to maintain the current bank angle (even if 0). That doesn't mean that the airplane can instantly respond. It is still a large heavy wing with inertia to overcome. If rolling into or out of a turn, centering the sidestick does not instantly stop the roll motion. It is still possible to get a pilot induced oscillation by moving the sidestick in a fashion that the airplane simply can't keep up with.

In Alternate 2 the roll axis is in direct aileron and spoiler control, with increased roll sensitivity. Two pair of spoilers are disabled to help keep the roll rates from becoming excessive. In Alternate 2, it is completely the pilot's job to maintain the desired bank angle. The airplane will not counteract any external forces (such as turbulence) that may tend to change the bank angle. We see evidence of this in the first few seconds after the autopilot disconnected, where the bank changed from wings level to 11° right without pilot inputs.

There is no annunciation telling which version of Alternate Law is active. Perhaps there should be due to the differences cited above. However, from the pilot's point of view it is virtually the same: if the bank angle is not what is desired, he must correct it. In Alternate Law, all maneuvering should be done with care. The difference is that Alternate 2 will require more pilot attention.

Bonin's 30 second initial fight for control in the roll axis, with what appears to be some pilot induced oscillation, may have diverted his attention from the pitch control, which eventually led to the stall and loss of control.

In both versions of Alternate Law, the pitch control law is exactly the same as in Normal Law (g-load demand). However, the flight control law may mask what the elevator is doing, because the elevator can move independently of the sidestick—because the pilot is not commanding elevator position, but g load. I believe this to be a key point in understanding how the airplane became so deeply stalled. If the protections are lost, even in the case of a stall the airplane wants to maintain the same g load. The normal pitching-down action, associated with positively stable civilian aircraft when below the desired speed, is counteracted by the flight control law's attempt to maintain the commanded g load. When the g load was lessened by an increasing descent rate due to the stalled condition, the elevator/stabilizer added more nose-up input in an attempt to compensate, which caused the descent rate to increase further.

Take a look at this section of the flight data recorder tracings outlined in blue showing g load, sidestick position, elevator, and stab position:

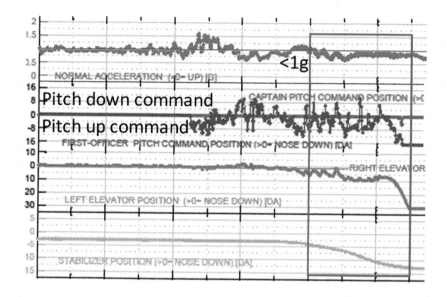

Note how the g load is less than 1. The sidestick commanded a pitch up (below the line commands a g load greater than 1). While the elevator position remained virtually unchanged, the stabilizer position was actively driving more nose-up for a total nose-up input greater than a direct sidestick-to-elevator relationship. At the right side of the outlined excerpt, the stabilizer was near its full-up position which left the elevator alone trying to fulfill the g-load command.

In another example, the elevator position is full up for a great deal of time near the end of the flight, despite the sidestick NOT being full up. At this point the descent rate had stabilized at approximately 12,000 ft/min, and the g load was approximately 1g. There were long periods of time where the pilot had moved the sidestick back, but not fully back, but the elevator was full up anyway. This was because the sidestick does not command elevator position, but g load. The elevator was trying to satisfy a g-load demand of greater than one and was doing everything it could to do so. The only thing it could do to increase the g load was more up elevator!

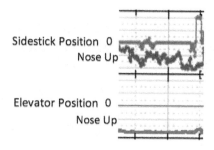

The full-up elevator was in addition to the stab position being full nose up at this time as well. A full-up stabilizer position will also reduce the elevator's pitch-down authority. Therefore, for a successful recovery with a full nose up stabilizer, a pitch down command for a longer period of time might be required. In extreme cases the pilot may have to manually move to trim to gain back pitch-down authority. The application of TOGA thrust (and its associated pitch-up moment) will also slow any pitch down action, as the engine's thrust vector would be acting in the opposite direction of the elevator's limited pitch down moment.

The elevator reached full nose up about the time that the AOA exceeded 30°. The airplane was falling (no better word to describe it) at a constant rate, and therefore maintaining about 1 g. Sidestick displacements were causing some elevator movements, but they were not held long enough to successfully reduce the angle of attack, which increased to 45°. While there is no guarantee that a recovery was possible (the final report states that it was not recoverable at this point), full nose down control, for as long as it takes, was required to reduce the angle of attack.

Manual resetting of the stabilizer trim might also have been required. In this case, full nose down control was only commanded once, and then only for two to three seconds, until the airplane was passing below 10,000 feet when two other short bursts were input. Once the stabilizer reached the full nose-up position, it stayed there (or very near there) for the remainder of the flight.

In roll, the flight controls were in Direct Law. But the airplane was fully stalled, essentially falling like a maple leaf. It is amazing it did not flip over or enter a spin. In the flight recorder tracing below, notice the roll angle (on top in blue) verses the sidestick and aileron position (brown and two shades of blue at the bottom).

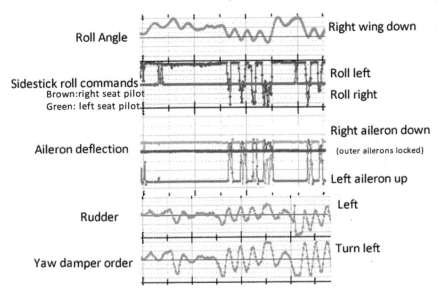

It is clear to see the direct relationship between sidestick position and aileron position (demonstrating the Alternate 2 Law roll mode: Direct) and long periods where the sidestick and the ailerons were at full deflection. At the same time, the bank angle was oscillating, showing the relative ineffectiveness of the ailerons. The inboard ailerons are the only ones used in this phase of flight. Outboard ailerons are locked out for pilot inputs when the airspeed is above 190 knots and flaps are up.

During this same time, the yaw damper was driving the rudder fighting left and right yaw motions, which may have been the only thing keeping the airplane close to upright.

Don't Forget to Fly the Airplane

In January 2013, the FAA released a Safety Alert for airline operators titled *Manual Flight Operations*,[41] reminding them that "maintaining and improving the knowledge and skills for manual flight operations is necessary for safe flight operations."

The alert continued: "Modern aircraft are commonly operated using autoflight systems (e.g., autopilot or autothrottle/autothrust). Unfortunately, continuous use of those systems does not reinforce a pilot's knowledge and skills in manual flight operations. Autoflight systems are useful tools for pilots and have improved safety and workload management, and thus enabled more precise operations. However, continuous use of autoflight systems could lead to degradation of the pilot's ability to quickly recover the aircraft from an undesired state."

In other words: pilots must continue to hand fly the airplane on a regular basis in order to keep those skills sharp, so that when the automatic systems are not working, they are able to!

The alert urges airlines to incorporate emphasis of manual flight operations into both line operations and training (initial/upgrade and recurrent), and develop policies that ensure there are opportunities for pilots to exercise manual flying skills at appropriate times.

Pilots need to be ready to take over not just in case of failure, but when the automation is not maneuvering the airplane as desired. This may be due to a programming error, that the automation is being too gentle when a faster response is desired, or that it is just easier to click the autopilot off for a few seconds to get what you need. I have delivered the following admonition to my students many times: "If it isn't doing what you want it to, click it off and make it do it!"

However, the more a pilot uses the automation, the less he and his fellow crewmembers may be willing to do without it. In fact, the less likely he may be *able* to do without it.

---

41   ww.faa.gov/other_visit/aviation_industry/airline_operators/airline_safety/ safo/all_safos/media/2013/SAFO13002.pdf

Just like driving a car with an automatic transmission for decades might cause a driver to lose their skill with a stickshift and clutch, a pilot's skills at flying solely on basic instruments can also suffer from non-use, even though he may have been quite skilled at one time.

A study of 30 airline pilots from a major US airline found significant deterioration of raw instrument flying skills over time while flying highly automated airplanes.[42]

A wide range of pilots were included in the study, both captains and first officers of wide-body and narrow-body aircraft with in-seat experience between two and 16 years.

The study had the pilots perform five maneuvers solely by reference to basic instruments (without flight directors, autopilot, autothrust, or moving map display): takeoff, takeoff with engine failure at V_1, holding, ILS approach, and a missed approach.

The average grade for each maneuver was below the ATP (Airline Transport Pilot) standards and closer to the instrument rating level. The poorest performance was seen on the holding maneuver. There was no significant performance difference between the pilots of narrow body airplanes, which tend to have more frequent take off and landing operations, and those of wide body airplanes, which tend to have had more experience yet fly fewer takeoff and landings.

The study revealed that the pilots' actual performance were lower than their expected level of performance in a pre-assessment survey. It may also be worth considering that only pilots who were fairly confident in their abilities might be willing to participate in such a study.

It is clear that when manual instrument flying is required, pilots who are less competent at manual instrument flying will require more concentration to maintain basic control of the airplane. Pilots who are more competent at those skills can spend less attention and cognitive

---

42   Degradation of Pilot Skills, Graduate Thesis, University of North Dakota, Michael W. Gillen, December 2008

function simply flying the airplane and more time on the problem at hand.

The study highlights the fact that even pilots who were extremely competent at hand flown instrument flight at one time, will see their skills deteriorate over time with non use. For pilots who spent a large portion of their career with advanced automation, those raw skills may not have been well developed to begin with.

Despite the time and effort required in training for pilots to become proficient with the complex automatic systems, there is still some hand flying done in training and checking. However, manual flying in the simulator for hand-flown maneuvers such as stalls and unusual attitude recovery is usually preceded with "OK, now we're going to do stalls or unusual attitude recovery." That, of course is not how the real-life crisis situations develop.

One maneuver that comes close to the transition from fully automated to fully manual (or nearly so) is the PRM approach breakout maneuver. A PRM approach is a Precision Runway Monitored approach used at some airports that have approaches on closely spaced parallel runways. Because the approaches are closely spaced, a dedicated air traffic controller monitors the approach and will give breakout instructions to the aircraft on one approach should an aircraft on the adjacent approach start to stray toward them. These breakout maneuvers are practiced in the simulator so that crews are able to perform them at the few congested airports that use them. Pilots will pre-brief the event, go into the simulator, and begin the approach knowing exactly what is to take place.

The breakout instructions will include a turn and may also include a climb or descent instructions. The maneuver is to be flown with the autopilot off to ensure that the clearance is complied with promptly. Therefore, the clearance requires the pilot to transition from a fully automated approach configuration, turn off the autopilot and flight director, initiate a turn to a given heading and comply with an altitude clearance. The maneuver requires prompt compliance but only normal bank angles and vertical speeds. It is even suggested that the airplane's configuration (landing gear and flaps) remain unchanged until established on the new heading and workload is reduced. During this maneuver, the autothrust may remain on, and will automatically maintain the selected speed, further reducing the workload.

However, this simple maneuver proves to be surprisingly challenging. My own informal survey finds that very few found the maneuver easy, and at least half needed to repeat the maneuver one or more times. Overcontrolling pitch or roll, and difficulty attaining and holding a pitch attitude, heading, or altitude were cited by instructors as common issues. Yet, it is only a taste of a real-life failure situation when the automation, including the autothrust, suddenly and unexpectedly shuts off.

Pilots, ask yourselves: How is your instrument scan? How well can you hold and make changes to heading, altitude, and airspeed without the flight director?

Will your hand flying skills be ready on your next flight when it is dark and bumpy, you are half tired, and things stop working?

Automation is great, but do not let yourself become automation dependent. No matter how good you were at one time, those skills have been shown to degrade over time if not practiced.

When hand flying, every pilot should deliberately practice precisely flying the attitude, airspeed, heading and altitude. Chances are, when the automation fails and manual flying is required, it will not be on a clear blue day.

Safe Harbor Concept

The Air Safety committee of the Air Line Pilots Association (ALPA) has introduced the concept of establishing a "safe harbor" technique to cope with "automation exceptions."

The committee recognized that even highly skilled instrument pilots lose perishable instrument flying skills as a result of continual reliance on automated systems. Also, new entrant pilots trained from inception utilizing glass cockpit instrumentation do not develop deeply embedded skills necessary for basic attitude instrument flying (a method of instrument flying based on setting and adjusting attitude and power setting, without the aid of any automation).

The concept of an automation exception involves not just failures but any situation where the automatic systems no longer provide appropriate guidance. This may include such situations as:

- Pitot-static errors including: icing (AF447), insect debris, mud-dauber nests, taped over static ports, water ingestion, hardware failures
- Software conflicts
- ATC requests, traffic avoidance maneuvers, PRM (Precision Runway Monitored) approach breakouts, go-arounds, etc.

In addition to these factors, other factors in loss of control incidents include environmental, systems induced failures, and the greatest contributor: pilot induced issues.

It is recognized that years of automatic operations or practicing hand flying but still following the flight director, have made it almost impossible for the pilot to doubt, disregard, or fly in opposition to displayed guidance. This automation addiction in combination with an automation exception sets up a critical window where the pilot must take positive action to maintain control of the airplane.

The paper, *Defining Commercial Transport Loss-of-Control: A Quantitative Approach* by James Wilborn and John Foster (a joint Boeing and NASA effort) studied six in-flight loss of control accidents and incidents that occurred between 1992 and 1996 due to a variety of causal factors. Whether a flight experienced a loss of control was determined by analyzing if the flight exceeded more than three out of five parameter envelopes rather than just a subjective evaluation. The envelopes related to flight dynamics, aerodynamics, structural integrity, and flight control use. Each of the five envelopes plot two parameters against each other relating the normal ranges of: AOA, sideslip angle, pitch and roll attitudes, load factor, airspeed, and pitch and roll attitudes with the trends of each factored against the pilot's control inputs.

They defined the interval between the time of the first envelope excursion and the time when control was lost as the critical window. In the six situations analyzed the average time available to the flight crew to provide a corrective response was 7.6 seconds. Therefore, the stabilization of the aircraft was found to be time-critical.

Compare this short time window with the flight data from AF447. Within the first two seconds the bank angle had increased to 8° right with no pilot input. At that point manual flying began with up to ¾ nose-up and up to full left roll input by the pilot flying. The first stall warning triggered six seconds after the disconnection and only three seconds after manual inputs began. Within the first 11 seconds of manual flight, the pitch attitude increased to 11°, the vertical speed to 5,200 feet per minute, and the g load reached 1.6g's in response to pilot inputs. At that time the airplane was established on a trajectory to rapidly gain altitude and lose precious airspeed. This led to a deeply stalled condition and complete loss of control only a minute later. By my estimation, recovery was possible at least within that one minute. However, as that minute progressed, more and more deliberate corrective action was required.

Within a few seconds of the autopilot disconnecting at 02:10:05, there were repeated excursions of the Dynamic Roll Control envelope, which plots pilot inputs against airplane response. The envelope was exceeded because the airplane's rolling motions were exactly out of sync with the sidestick lateral commands. In the pitch axis, even though the pilot's pitch inputs were inappropriate, the airplane was responding to them and therefore was not in violation of the Dynamic Pitch Control envelope. By 02:10:51 the roll had stabilized, but the stall warning activated which violated one parameter on each of two related envelopes (AOA and speed).

By 02:11:31 the airplane was officially out of control. The AOA was excessively high, the airspeed excessively low. Pitch response was poor at best, and roll control was non-existent. It was at that time that First Officer Bonin declared, "I don't have control of the airplane any more now." It had exceeded four of the five loss-of-control envelopes: Adverse Aerodynamics, Dynamic Pitch control, Dynamic Roll Control, and Structural Integrity. The Unusual Attitude envelope was the only one not exceeded, as the pitch and bank angles did not reach the boundaries of that envelope.

The safe harbor technique is a tool that can be applied quickly to prevent an automation exception from progressing to a loss of control. It involves first turning off automation (autopilot, flight director, and autothrust), this removes any distractions and disengages inappropriate modes. Then the pilot flies a known (memorized) pitch and power setting for level flight. Once the airplane is firmly under control, the exception condition can be dealt with and conditions permitting, automation reestablished in an orderly manner.

747 Captain Dennis Landry, promoter of the Safe Harbor concept, offers the following analogy:

> When we were kids we could all ride a bike really well. We often rode with "no hands" and could talk with our friends while navigating streets full of potholes. At that point we were "ATP skilled" bike-riders. But when we reached driving age, we found cars to be way cooler. "Glass Cockpits" are similar: no more bike riding or "Steam Gauge" flying for me. We stuck the bike on the roof of the car just in case the car ever broke down.
>
> What if, fifteen years later on a dark lonely night in bad weather, the car breaks down? No worries: we still have a bike strapped to the roof. Never mind that we have not ridden it for 15 years, WE can RIDE! Well, you start down a steep hill and as you attempt to turn the bike the handle bars come off. When you were 16 and an "ATP skill level" bike rider this would have been fun. But now it's a whole lot less enjoyable.

Maintaining hand flying skills to be able to competently handle emergency flight with an automation exception requires practice. Hand flying by following the flight director, while common, is not adequate preparation for the full instrument scan required during an unplanned automation exception event. That practice should be made under safe conditions such as only day, visual conditions, in low workload environments (10,000–25,000 feet), and with a briefing to fellow crewmembers beforehand.

This work by ALPA is ongoing and will hopefully become a routine part of regular training and practice in line flying to mitigate automation addiction.

Flight Directors

It is not 100% clear that the AF447 pilots followed the flight directors when they reappeared after the autopilot disconnected, but it looks like a distinct possibility.

What is clear about the flight directors is that except for a few seconds, from the time the autopilot disconnected, they were providing inappropriate guidance.

The flight directors automatically disappeared due to disagreeing air data (airspeed), but remained selected on. When two sources of air data agreed again, they reappeared in heading and vertical speed mode, which is the default mode for the flight director or autopilot to engage in when neither are already on.

The vertical speed when they came back on was very high, initially 1,400 feet per minute, then later 6,000 feet per minute. Therefore, that was the target vertical speed that they provided guidance to maintain.

The flight directors are a very powerful cue. It is easy to rely on them with little awareness of what attitude they are commanding. Following the flight directors does not relieve the pilot of the responsibility to ensure the guidance they are providing is appropriate.

For a low-time pilot like FO Bonin, who probably rarely hand flew the airplane, it is likely that when they reappeared he tried to follow them.

This may be the reason that First Officer Robert was telling Bonin that he was going up, and Bonin seemed confused as to whether he was climbing or not. The airplane was able to perform the high climb rates initially commanded by the flight director; however, as speed decayed, it became impossible to do so.

The first steps in the unreliable airspeed procedure, and a memory item, are to turn off the flight directors (and the autopilot and autothrust, if not already off). If not selected off, the flight directors can reappear on their own (and in an inappropriate mode). The Flight Mode Annunciator (FMA) will display the current flight director mode, but it is easy to miss when things are busy. The autopilot and autothrust will not re-engage on their own, only the flight director will. Pilots should then re-engage the automatic systems only when the air data has been confirmed correct (e.g., by reference to performance tables).

One of the recommendations of the investigation was that flight directors should not automatically re-engage once they disappear, but should require explicit pilot selection to be re-engaged (like the autopilot). This would have prevented their redisplay in AF447's steep climb, where the flight directors provided inappropriate guidance to continue the climb at high vertical speeds. There are several situations, besides data loss, that can trigger the flight directors to disappear.

Training Matters

Training and experience matters a great deal in producing pilots that can handle these or other unexpected situations.

For these high performance airplanes, training exercises need to demonstrate and compare the stall margins and recovery techniques in both high and low altitude regimes.

At low altitude, high angles of attack are required for stall, and power addition provides a quick recovery with minimal loss of altitude.

Contrast that with the high altitude scenario, where the stall margin is very narrow, and power addition can be weak or ineffective in reducing the angle of attack, and in some cases may actually hamper the ability to pitch the airplane down. In this environment, altitude will *have to* be traded to gain airspeed. The performance physics simply do not allow the airplane to regain airspeed in level flight with the available power once it has gotten critically slow. Additionally, as the recovery progresses, and Mach number increases the airplane's stall margin again decreases. Therefore, the recovery must be made somewhat gently to prevent a secondary stall encounter in the recovery.

The idiosyncrasies of fly-by-wire airplanes must be demonstrated and understood, not just mentioned in a briefing. In this case the absence of angle-of-attack protection and low speed stabilities, the function of the auto-trim, and the fact that the airplane's natural dynamic stability to pitch down was masked by the g-load demand system are key to understanding the handling of the airplane in these situations. For the airplane to pitch down, in situations where the fly-by-wire stabilities are lost, requires the pilot to push forward on the sidestick. These are key concepts of the airplane that should not be glossed over. Pilots do not intuitively know this. When I have demonstrated these factors to crews in training, numerous pilots stated that this was the most informative simulator session they have ever had.

Training in these areas has improved since the accident, due in part to the findings of the accident, as it brought to light some areas of misunderstanding.

The background of a pilot can also make a difference. First Officer Bonin came up through an *ab initio* program on the airline fast track. I am sure stalls were taught and demonstrated, but the training may not have been extensive. Most of his flight career was probably spent in cruise flight with a heavy use of automation. Despite almost 3,000 hours total time, his actual hands on time of *actively flying* the airplane may have been minimal.

Contrast that with a pilot who worked as a flight instructor *teaching* stalls recovery or spin training. Graduates of military training programs also receive intense instruction in maneuvers and awareness of angle of attack and the effects of high altitude and high speed aerodynamics, as well as a very wide envelope of attitudes. Also skilled are pilots with many hours on airplanes where hand flying was required due less sophisticated autopilots or none at all.

Pilots who have come up through *ab initio* programs may have missed much of this experience. Training programs and company policies need to be aware of this and include hand flying in initial and recurrent training, as well as support hand flying the airplane during routine operations where practical.

An A320 Captain relates the following story of a pitot-static problem he encountered in an A320. The incident follows the probable contamination of the static ports during a washing, which was then addressed by maintenance before departure.

> We had just punched into the overcast and raised the flaps when the stall warning sounded and the flight control system went to alternate law indicated on the PFD. I had the first officer lower the nose immediately and cobbed the power. (We were above Point Loma by now and had nothing but ocean ahead of us—a stall recovery maneuver was not an option) There were no ECAM messages during this entire scenario. I immediately looked at the FO's airspeed to see what it said because the water in the system was still on my mind. I then checked the backup instruments to see what the airspeed was indicating. All three were within about five knots so the puzzle was raised a couple of degrees in my mind. What was the real airspeed? When we broke out on top about a minute later I could visually tell that we were hauling so I knew we were above stall speed and the attitude was nowhere near stall attitude. The warning stayed on till about 275K and we kept the airspeed there till we came up with a plan.

He attributes his ability to maintain control, verify indications with the standby system, and successfully land the airplane in instrument conditions to his extensive hand flying experience in the Navy and on the DC-9.

Good training helps to reinforce or strengthen those skills. But good training does not happen on its own. It takes a training program that is willing to provide the training needed, even if it means going beyond the regulatory requirements, and it takes good instructors to make it happen effectively.

Good instructors can detect signs of pilot misunderstanding. The cues are often subtle: how students move the controls, what modes they select, how they plan their energy management on approach, when they change configuration and much more. Then, the instructor can try to fill in the holes in a pilot's experience or understanding with exercises to improve his understanding and skill.

A threat to this system is the increasing use of instructors with no experience in the airplane they are teaching in, especially in later stages of training. They set up the simulator as per the syllabus, perform the maneuvers listed in the lesson to the standards prescribed, but may lack the experience and ability to catch the hints of misunderstanding subtly displayed by the student. Their lack of actual line flying experience can sometimes allow them to miss the significance of certain items as it would apply to real life scenarios. Will their students be ready if real life strays from the cookbook procedure?

Sitting and watching the autopilot fly the airplane, following flight directors with little awareness of what pitch attitude to fly should they disappear, are behaviors that despite adding hours to a logbook, add little to a pilot's real experience and ability to be the defining factor between a failure and tragedy.

The AF447 final report[43] validates these assertions with the findings of Air France's own internal safety report. Among the findings:

- The piloting abilities of long-haul and/or *ab initio* pilots were sometimes poor;
- A notable loss of good sense and general aeronautical knowledge;
- Weaknesses in terms of representation and awareness of the

---

43   AF447 Final Accident Report page 192

situation during system failures (reality, severity, danger level, induced effects …).

It does not take a great deal of imagination to apply these findings to the crew of AF447. It is sad to consider that these are probably not the only three pilots incapable of handling this situation. Though the empirical evidence indicates they are the minority, as the dependence on technology and economics change the nature of pilot training, we must consider what the future will bring. Training departments at all airlines must take these factors into account.

Chapter 11: Going Forward

It would be easy to simply criticize the incompetence of the two first officers, but it is not as simple as that. The vast majority of accidents have multiple causes. Air France 447 is no exception.

The loss of the autopilot, autothrust, and airspeed indications, occurring in turbulent weather at night was combined with degraded flight controls, and flight directors that provided inappropriate guidance. The situation was beyond the ability of the crew to:

- Recognize what had happened
- Recognize what was happening
- Determine what actions to take to restore controlled flight

But, the skills of the two first officers were a product of their prior training and experience.

Not long ago, hand flying was common. Operating today's highly automated aircraft virtually 100% of the time with the automation engaged has allowed manually flying skills to erode to the point where they may not be sufficient to handle an emergency. We must also recognize that a generation of pilots have been trained on the techniques of following the flight director, and the development of high-level manual flying skills have been de-emphasized.

If we fail to train our fellow pilots to manually fly the airplane under the most challenging conditions then we have failed them, our passengers, and cabin crew. In the absence of this training, any significant loss of autoflight systems or degradation of flight controls could result in a scenario for which they are not prepared. Which is a recipe for another disaster.

Analysis of the factors involved reveals numerous areas of pilot misinterpretation and misunderstanding. This fact alone should make us resolve to do a better job in educating our pilot population. These factors include:

- How to properly operate the weather radar to account for the low radar reflectivity of storms in the ITCZ.
- The proper pitch attitude and power setting to maintain or reestablish cruise flight.
- That Alternate Law provided no protections, could maintain a dangerously high pitch attitude with no back pressure at all, and provided nearly double the normal roll response to sidestick input.
- That the synthetic voice announcing "STALL, STALL, STALL" meant that the nose must be pitched down, as it would not happen on its own.
- That insufficient power exists at cruise altitude to constitute a stall recovery.
- A misidentification of the stall buffet for a high speed buffet. Believing they had "some crazy speed" the pilot flying even deployed the speed brakes momentarily, unaware that the wing on this airplane made Mach buffet extremely unlikely or perhaps not even possible.
- Both first officers lost the discipline of accomplishing the abnormal procedure, and failed to identify who was flying the airplane. The synthetic voice announced "DUAL INPUT" while both pilots were trying to fly the airplane, sometimes with conflicting commands.

But as egregious as all these error seem, and indeed were, we must realize that these pilots were the product of their training and experience, as are we all. Like the loyal family dog who lets in the burglar, one cannot truly be expected to effectively handle a crisis situation for which they have not been trained.

However, even the skills of pilots with extensive manual instrument flying experience will erode over time when those skills are not maintained with practice.

We must, therefore train our fellow airmen:

- To be able to handle the hand flying that the autopilot relieves them of
- To be aware of the normal pitch attitudes and power settings that the flight directors and autothrust allow them to forget or never learn
- To understand the weather they are surrounded by
- To understand the aerodynamics that keep them aloft and
- To understand the unique characteristics of their aircraft

We must not allow mastery of the Flight Management System to be confused with airmanship.

It is our sacred duty to each other and to every passenger that ever climbs aboard.

We have been warned.

Appendix

Recommendations of the Investigation

The BEA released a number of safety recommendations in the various reports on the accident. These cover a range of subjects from airplane an simulator design to search and rescue. In the final report they are grouped primarily by which report the recommendations were issued in. I have arranged them below by subject.

Flight Recorders

Extend as rapidly as possible from 30 to 90 days the regulatory transmission time for Underwater Locator Beacons (ULBs) installed on flight recorders on airplanes performing public transport flights over maritime areas; make it mandatory, as rapidly as possible, for airplanes performing public transport flights over maritime areas to be equipped with an additional ULB capable of transmitting on a frequency (for example between 8.5 kHz and 9.5 kHz) and for a duration adapted to the prelocalization of wreckage;

Study the possibility of making it mandatory for airplanes performing public transport flights to regularly transmit basic flight parameters (for example position, altitude, speed, heading).

Ask the FLIRECP (ICAO Flight Recorder Panel) group to establish proposals on the conditions for implementing deployable recorders of the Eurocae ED-112 type for airplanes performing public transport flights.

That ICAO require that aircraft undertaking public transport flights with passengers be equipped with an image recorder that makes it possible to observe the whole of the instrument panel; and that at the same time,

ICAO establish very strict rules for the readout of such recordings in order to guarantee the confidentiality of the recordings.

Today, the regulation requires recording of the flight parameters displayed on the left side. Some parameters essential to the analysis of the conduct of the flight are lacking, in particular those displayed to the pilot in the right seat: speed, altitude, attitudes, position of the flight director crossbars, etc. In addition, airplanes are equipped with complex systems whose functional analysis is limited and delayed by the absence of a recording of all of the data sources that they use.

Consequently, the BEA recommends: that EASA and the FAA make mandatory the recording:

- of the position of the flight director crossbars
- of the parameters relating to the conduct of the flight displayed on the right side, in addition to those displayed on the left side

And that EASA and the FAA evaluate the relevance of making mandatory the recording of the air data and inertial parameters of all of the sources used by the systems.

That EASA and ICAO make mandatory as quickly as possible, for airplanes making public transport flights with passengers over maritime or remote areas, triggering of data transmission to facilitate localization as soon as an emergency situation is detected on board;

And that EASA and ICAO study the possibility of making mandatory, for airplanes making public transport flights with passengers over maritime or remote areas, the activation of the emergency locator transmitter (ELT), as soon as an emergency situation is detected on board.

Certification

Undertake studies to determine with appropriate precision the composition of cloud masses at high altitude; and in coordination with the other regulatory authorities, based on the results obtained, to modify the certification criteria.

That EASA and the FAA evaluate the relevance of requiring the presence of an angle of attack indicator directly accessible to pilots on board airplanes.

Training for Manual Aircraft Handling

That EASA review the content of check and training programs and make mandatory, in particular, the setting up of specific and regular exercises dedicated to manual aircraft handling of approach to stall and stall recovery, including at high altitude.

That EASA define additional criteria for access to the role of relief captain so as to ensure better task-sharing in case of augmented crews; and that, provisionally, the DGAC define additional criteria for access to the role of relief captain so as to ensure better task-sharing in case of augmented crews.

Search and Rescue

ICAO ensure the implementation of SAR coordination plans or regional protocols covering all of the maritime or remote areas for which international coordination would be required in the application of SAR procedures, including in the South Atlantic area.

The DGAC, in concert with the other services responsible, develop a homogeneous framework for training and for approval of operators responsible for search and rescue activities in France.

ICAO define the framework for the training of SAR operators in its standards and recommended practices.

Within France: the DGAC designate a point of contact at ICAO for the ARCC that has adequate means to accomplish his/her missions.

ICAO ensure each Member State has a national point of contact and makes his/her contact information available.

ICAO amend Annex 12 on search and rescue operations so as to encourage contracting states to equip their search aircraft with buoys to measure drift and to drop them, when these units are involved in the search for persons lost at sea.

Air Traffic Control

The Brazilian and Senegalese authorities make mandatory the utilization, by airplanes so equipped, of ADS-C and CPDLC functions in the zones in question.

ICAO request the involved States to accelerate the operational implementation of air traffic control and communication systems that allow a permanent and reliable link to be made between ground and airplane in all of the areas where HF remains the only means of communication between the ground and airplanes.

Pilot Training

EASA ensure the integration, in type rating and recurrent training programs, of exercises that take into account all of the reconfiguration laws. The objective sought is to make its recognition and understanding easier for crews especially when dealing with the level of protection available and the possible differences in handling characteristics, including at the limits of the flight envelope.

More generally, EASA ensure that type rating and recurrent training programs take into account the specificities of the aircraft for which they are designed.

EASA define recurrent training program requirements to make sure, through practical exercises, that the theoretical knowledge, particularly on flight mechanics, is well understood.

EASA review the requirements for initial, recurrent and type rating training for pilots in order to develop and maintain a capacity to manage crew resources when faced with the surprise generated by unexpected situations.

EASA ensure that operators reinforce CRM training to enable

acquisition and maintenance of adequate behavioral automatic responses in unexpected and unusual situations with a highly charged emotional factor.

EASA define criteria for selection and recurrent training among instructors that would allow a high and standardized level of instruction to be reached.

Flight Simulators

EASA modify the basis of the regulations in order to ensure better fidelity for simulators in reproducing realistic scenarios of abnormal situations.

EASA ensure the introduction into the training scenarios of the effects of surprise in order to train pilots to face these phenomena and to work in situations with a highly charged emotional factor.

Ergonomics

EASA require a review of the re-display and reconnection logic of the flight directors after their disappearance, in particular to review the conditions in which an action by the crew would be necessary to re-engage them.

Further, even if it is not sure that the crew followed the orders from the flight director while the stall warning was active, the orders from the crossbars were in contradiction with the inputs to make in this situation and thus may have troubled the crew.

Consequently, the BEA recommends that: EASA require a review of the functional or display logic of the flight director so that it disappears or presents appropriate orders when the stall warning is triggered.

In so much as certain on-board systems identified the problem, but the alerts presented to the crew only presented the symptoms:

EASA study the relevance of having a dedicated warning provided to the crew when specific monitoring is triggered, in order to facilitate comprehension of the situation.

EASA determine the conditions in which, on approach to stall, the presence of dedicated visual indications, combined with an aural warning should be made mandatory.

When airspeeds are below 60 kt, the stall warning is no longer available, even though it may be beneficial for it to be available at all times.

Consequently, the BEA recommends that: EASA require a review of the conditions for the functioning of the stall warning in flight when speed measurements are very low.

Operational and Technical Feedback

EASA improve the feedback process by making mandatory the operational and human factors analysis of in-service events in order to improve procedures and the content of training programs.

Specifically, that the DGAC take steps aimed at improving the relevance and the quality of incident reports written by flight crews and their distribution, in particular to manufacturers.

Oversight of the Operator

In-flight and ground inspections by the Authority within the airline never brought to light any major deviations, whether in relation to the operator's conformity to the regulatory provisions, to the recurrent simulator training or in flight. Thus, the whole range of inspections did not bring to light the fragile nature of the CRM nor the weaknesses of the two copilots in manual airplane handling. Though respecting the regulatory requirements applicable to oversight, it appears that the organization, methods and means deployed by the authority were not adequate to detect the weaknesses of an operator and impose the necessary corrective measures.

Key Flight Recorder Parameters

The following is a collection of the key parameters from the flight recorder tracings provided by the final accident report.

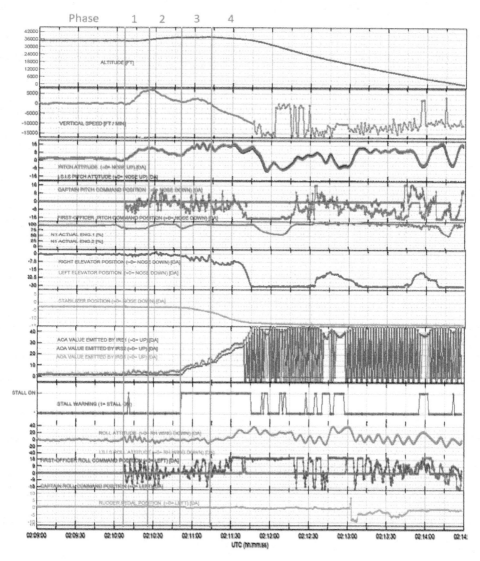

Glossary

Ab Initio - A Latin term meaning "from the beginning" whereby an airline often hires a pilot with minimal qualifications and provides the training necessary to serve as a flight officer.

ACARS - Aircraft Communications Addressing and Reporting System. A messaging system used to deliver messages between the aircraft and ground stations, and in some cases ATC.

ADIRS - Air Data Inertial Reference Systems Three systems comprised of the Air Data and Inertial reference components.

ADS-C - Automatic Dependent Surveillance - Contract. An automatic position reporting system widely used in oceanic areas where radar is not available.

ADR - Air Data Reference. Three systems that provide altitude and airspeed data.

AOA -Angle of attack. The angle between the wing and the relative wind (the apparent wind resulting from the forward motion of the airplane)

ARCC - Aeronautical Rescue Coordination Centre

ATC - Air Traffic Control

BEA - Bureau d'Enquêtes et d'Analyses pour la sécurité de l'aviation civile (Office of Investigations and Analysis for the safety of civil aviation

CG - Center of Gravity

CPDLC - Controller Pilot Data Link Communications. A system for sending and receiving text messages between the aircraft and ATC that ensures the accuracy of the transmitted data. It is widely used in, though not limited to, oceanic areas where VHF radio coverage is not available.

CRM - Crew Resource Management (formerly Cockpit Resource

Management). A human factors approach to more effectively managing of the flight, which makes optimum use of all available resources— equipment, procedures and people—to promote safety and enhance the efficiency of operations.

CVR - Cockpit Voice Recorder. This recorder provides a multi-channel recording of radio, interphone, and other communications from each pilot station, and cockpit area microphone audio, for use in accident investigations. Maximum storage capacity is between 30 minutes and 2 hours.

DFDR - Digital Flight Data Recorder. This recorder constantly records several thousand aircraft parameters for use in accident investigations.

DGAC - Direction Generale de l'Aviation civile (French Director General of Civil Aviation)

EASA - European Aviation Safety Agency. The Agency promotes the highest common standards of safety and environmental protection in civil aviation in Europe and worldwide. It is the centerpiece of a new regulatory system which provides for a single European market in the aviation industry.

ECAM - Electronic Centralized Aircraft Monitor. This system provides display and monitoring of aircraft systems. It uses the two center display screens on the instrument panel, and includes alerts, non-normal checklists, and other information.

ELT - Emergency Locator Transmitter. A transmitter that sends an emergency location signal (trackable by satellite and search and rescue personnel). ELTs are typically triggered automatically by impact forces.

FCPC - Flight Control Primary Computer (PRIM)

Flight Director - A display, on the A330 consisting of a horizontal and a vertical command bars on the primary flight display (PFD). The command bars are generated by the flight management computer and provide pitch and roll guidance to the pilot to follow identical to the commands the autopilot follows when it is on. The FD and autopilot are usually both on in flight.

FO - First Officer

FPV - Flight Path Vector. A display on the PFD that shows the lateral and horizontal trajectory of the airplane independent of attitude.

GPWS - Ground Proximity Warning System

HF Radio - High Frequency radio. A radio spectrum (shortwave) that allows for long distance radio communications. It is widely used in oceanic areas where VHF radio coverage is not available. It is highly subject to interference and poor transmission quality.

ICAO - International Civil Aviation Organization. Promotes understanding and security through cooperative aviation regulation.

IR - Inertial Reference. Three systems that provide attitude, heading, position, and other inertial based data

Mach - In reference to a scale where Mach 1.0 equals the speed of sound.

N_1 - The speed of the fan stage of the engine, expressed in percent, though 100% is not the upper limit. It is the primary thrust setting parameter.

ND - Navigation Display. On the A330 this display includes a moving map display, weather radar, TCAS, terrain, and additional navigation data.

PIC - Pilot in Command

PF - Pilot Flying

PFD - Primary Flight Display. On the A330 this one display includes attitude, airspeed, heading, altitude, vertical speed, autoflight mode annunciations, and some additional information.

PNF - Pilot not Flying.

SAR - Search and Rescue.

SELCAL - Selective Calling. A system that allows the radio operator to transmit an aircraft's unique SELCAL code. When the radio receiver recognizes its code, it sounds a call signal in the cockpit alerting the crew to contact the radio operator for a message.

THS - Trimmable Horizontal Stabilizer. aka: stab

TOGA - Takeoff/Go Around: A thrust setting and the full forward thrust lever position. If selected in flight with the flaps are out, it also commands the autopilot/flight director system to provide go-around guidance.

ULB - Underwater Locator Beacon

VHF Radio - Very High Frequency radio. The common radio band used aeronautical radio transmission. The transmissions are usually of good quality, but are limited to line-of-sight transmissions, and are therefore unusable for long distance communications.

About the Author

Bill Palmer is a currently an A330 captain for an international airline.

As a member of his airline's A330 development team for the introduction of the airplane to its fleet, he has been intimately involved in A330 fleet since 2002. He was the lead author and editor for the airline's A330 systems manual, and has written numerous A330 training publications. He has served as an airplane and simulator instructor, check airman, designated examiner, and also on training related projects from video production to simulator certification.

Bill started flying at the age of 15, soloed on his 16th birthday and completed his private certificate at 17. He attended Embry-Riddle Aeronautical University and holds a BS in Aeronautical Science. He earned his flight instructor certificate in 1978 and has been instructing almost non-stop since then, while holding airplane, instrument, multi-engine, and ground instructor certificates. Besides light aircraft he has also taught on the 727, 757, A320, DC-10, and A330, and written manuals for the DC-10, A330, and B-787 fleets. He has also produced numerous training publications and videos for the various fleets as well.

Bill holds an ATP with type ratings in A320, A330, B757/767, B777, DC10, and commercial glider and flight engineer-turbojet ratings.

CPSIA information can be obtained
at www.ICGtesting.com
Printed in the USA
BVOW11s1131230218
508723BV00006B/78/P